LOOKING FOR WOLFGANG AMADEUS MOZART

WALTER M. WEISS

*Looking for
Wolfgang Amadeus*

MOZART

*A Travel Companion
Through
Salzburg, Prague & Vienna*

*Translated
by Diane Elphee*

VERLAG CHRISTIAN BRANDSTÄTTER

Contents

7   Chronological Table

50 Genealogical Tree of the Mozart, Pertl and Weber Families

52 Mozart's Travels

55 Salzburg
79 *Salzburg Facts*

85 Prague
109 *Prague Facts*

113 Vienna
154 *Vienna Facts*

159 More Mozart Memorials
170 *Memorials Facts*

172 Bibliography

175 Illustrations

City Maps
Salzburg: front leaf
Prague: page 86
Vienna: back leaf

X

CHRONOLOGICAL TABLE

Leopold Mozart (1719–1787), oil painting probably by Pietro Antonio Lorenzoni, c. 1765.

1719 Leopold Mozart was born in Augsburg (in the house Frauentorstraße 30) on November 14th, his father was a book-binder, his mother, a weaver's daughter.

1720 On Christmas Day Mozart's mother, Anna Maria, was born in St. Gilgen on Lake Wolfgang. She was the daughter of Wolfgang Nikolaus Pertl, the Archbishop's Commissioner, and Eva Rosina.

1737 Leopold moves to Salzburg, where he enrols at Salzburg's Benedictine University as a student of philosophy. Three years later he is appointed groom and musician by Johann Baptist Count Thurn-Valsassina.

The Salzach city's music life is influenced just as much by the cultural happenings in Venice, Mantua and Milan as it is by Vienna and Prague, and is about to reach the zenith of its long and great history. Many appraised and brilliant musicians, among them many Italians and Joseph Haydn's younger brother Michael (1737–1806), nurture, as employees of the representative Archbishop, the heritage of famous predecessors like Paul Hofhaimer, Georg Muffat and Heinrich Ignaz Biber. At the same time, away from court, there is an increase in the number of bourgeois instrumental- and vocal groups.

Johann Michael Haydn

Augsburg: Frauentorstraße, the birthplace of Leopold Mozart. Coloured engraving c. mid 18th century

ORIGIN

A view of Salzburg from the Kapuzinerberg. A coloured engraving by Aug. Franz Heinrich von Naumann in 1791, the year W.A. Mozart died.

1743   Leopold Mozart becomes 4th violinist in the Salzburg Archepiscopal Court Orchestra, which he is to remain in for the next 44 years. In the following year he is appointed the violin teacher of the "Kapellhausknaben" (choristers).

1747   On the 21st of November Leopold marries Anna Maria Pertl in the Salzburg Cathedral. The newly weds, who are considered the "prettiest couple in the whole of Salzburg", take a small, three-roomed apartment in the house of their friend and merchant Johann Lorenz Hagenauer on the Löchelplatz (today: Getreidegasse 9).

1751   The couple's first daughter, Maria Anna Walburg Ignatia, later known under the nickname of "Nannerl", is born on the 30th July.

1756   At 8 p.m. on the 27th of January, in the "Hagenauer house" third floor, Anna Maria Mozart gives birth to a boy. The christening of Johannes Chrysostomus Wolfgang Theophilus (Gottlieb) takes place next day in Salzburg Cathedral. The last of the four names was chosen in honour of the godfather Johann Gottlieb Pergmayr, – Senator, merchant and friend of the family –, and later changed to the Latin version of "Amadeus". Of Mozart's six siblings, two brothers and four sisters, only Nannerl is still alive.

In the summer of the same year Leopold, musician and pedagogue, has his violin teaching method published under the title of "Versuch einer gründlichen Violinschule" by the well-known Augsburg publisher,

Mozart's mother Maria Anna Mozart née Pertl (1720–1788). Painted c. 1775.

Wolfgang's beloved sister Maria Anna, known as "Nannerl". Painted by Pietro Antonio Lorenzoni, 1763.

The record of Wolfgangs baptism on the 28th January 1756 in the birth-register of Salzburg Cathedral.

Below: Title-page from the treatise "Violin School" by Leopold Mozart. Published in the year that Wolfgang was born

Johann Jakob Lotter. In the 18th century this was considered a fundamental educational treatise and as a consequence experiences many translations and printings. Leopold Mozart is also extremely active as a composer. He writes numerous Masses, oratorios, litanies, vespers, cantatas, arias, songs, symphonies, as well as piano and chamber music.

1758 On the 25th September in Augsburg Maria Anna Thekla, Wolfgang's cousin "Bäsle", is born. She goes down in musical history as authoress of the famous witty-rude Bäsle-letters.

1759 Leopold compiles a notebook for his eminently talented Nannerl "Pour le clavecin". It is soon to serve her younger brother as a learning aid.

1761 Nannerl's father writes an entry in her notebook: "Wolfgang has learned this menuet and trio in one half hour, just one day before his 5th birthday, on the 26th January at 10 p.m." The five-year-old's first works – one *andante* and one *allegro*, both in C major, are composed between February and April and also recorded in the notebook. At the beginning of September he makes his first public appearance on stage as a dancer in the Latin school comedy "Sigismundus Hungariae Rex" in the main hall of the University. In the corresponding text-book the name "Wolfangus Mozhart" can be seen.

Leopold Mozart – Title-page from his famous work "Violin School". Copper engraving by J. A. Friedrich, 1756.

Leopold Mozart (playing the violin) with his children, Nannerl (singing) and Wolfgang Amadeus (at the spinet) in Paris. An engraving by Jean Baptiste Delafosse according to an original by Louis Carrogis de Carmontelle, 1764.

SCHOOLING

1762 Wolfgang's future wife, Constanze Weber, is born in Zell in Wiesenthal on January the 5th. On the 12th of the same month Leopold travels with his daughter and son to Munich for three weeks, where they successfully perform for the Elector Maximilian III Joseph as child prodigies. In mid-September the family sets out, this time complete with their mother, on another tour. This trip leads through Passau, downstream on the Danube to Linz and Vienna and is the start of an intensive period of travelling which is to continue for many years to come. During this time the children give rise to astonishment and admiration at the courts of Europe as cembalo, violin and organ virtuosos, and Wolfgang as a young man, also as a conductor and a composer. The proud Papa and impresario feels it his duty "to announce a miracle to the world that has been born by God's grace in Salzburg. I am responsible to the Lord to act thus, otherwise I would be the most unthankful creature." During his short life Wolfgang will spend a total of more than 250 days in uncomfortable private carriages or stage-coaches.

Empress Maria Theresia. A portrait painted by the director of the Viennese Academy, Martin van Meytens, in 1759.

The children give their first concert in Vienna in the Palais Collalto on the square known as "Am Hof", on October 9th. Four days later the social climax of their stay comes: the Mozarts are "most graciously" received by Emperor Franz I and Maria Theresia for three hours in the Palace of Schönbrunn. Performances follow in the palaces of various aristocrats, among others at those of the family Colloredo-Mansfeld, Wilczek, Auersperg, Pálffy, Zinzendorf and Harrach. On the 31st October Leopold gives his son, as he had his daughter, a personally compiled notebook as a gift on his name-day.

1763 On January 5th, shortly after returning to Salzburg, Wolfgang falls ill for the first time with rheumatic fever. On the 9th of June, the father, the children and a servant begin their first big journey through Europe. The tour leads through Germany, Belgium and France to England, then, on the return trip, through Holland and Switzerland, and lasts a total of nearly three and a half years.

In Augsburg Wolfgang meets "Bäsle" for the first time. This is the lady he is to reveal himself to fifteen years later as an impulsive, obscene letter writer and onomatopoetic verbal Dadaist ("dreck, schmeck – dreck! – leck – o charmante! – dreck, leck! – das freüet mich!") (muck, suck – muck! – lick – o enchanting! – muck, lick! – I liketh that!).

In Schwetzingen the family from Salzburg hears the extremely famous Mannheim Orchestra for the first time. Leopold calls them "without doubt the best in the whole of Germany". In Frankfurt, Goethe, only fourteen-years-old himself, experiences a performance by the seven-year-old Wolfgang. He mentions in a letter to Eckermann nearly seventy years later that he remembers "the little man in hairdo and rapier quite clearly". The children appear in concert in Brussels for the Governor General of the Austrian Netherlands, Prince Karl Alexander von Lothringen. Paris is reached on the 18th of November.

Emperor Franz I, Maria Theresia and their children. The boy, in the red-gold court attire, in the midst of the eleven children is the 13-year-old, heir to the throne, Joseph. Painting by Martin van Meytens, c. 1754/55.

Music lovers but arch conservatives: the English Regents, George III and Charlotte Sophie, that receive the Mozarts in Buckingham Palace. Portraits by Johann Zoffany c. 1765.

1764   On New Year's Day, in the presence of Louis XV and the Polish Queen Maria Leszczýnska, the Mozarts take part at the royal dinner, the so-called "Grand Couvert", at the Palace of Versailles.

At the beginning of February, Wolfgang's Opus 1 appears in print – the *sonatas for piano* or *piano and violin K 6* and *7*. On the 27th of April, four days after arriving in London, the child prodigies are received by George III and his wife Charlotte Sophie at Buckingham Palace. Further performances are made for the musically extremely open-minded royal couple. At one festival concert given on the 19th May, which led to the acquaintance of the court music master, Johann Christian Bach, Wolfgang accompanies the Queen as she sings.

Stimulated by the lively intellectual climate in the city on the Thames, and the demand for instrumental music coming "from the amateurs", he composes his first symphonies at the turn of the New Year.

1765   The *sonatas for piano, violin* and *flute and cello (K 10–15)* are published and dedicated to the Queen of England. For a series of perfomances in the tavern "The Swan and Harp", that should better the family's financial situation after Leopold's illness, the first piano pieces are produced, amongst them the *piano sonata for four-hands (K 19d)*.

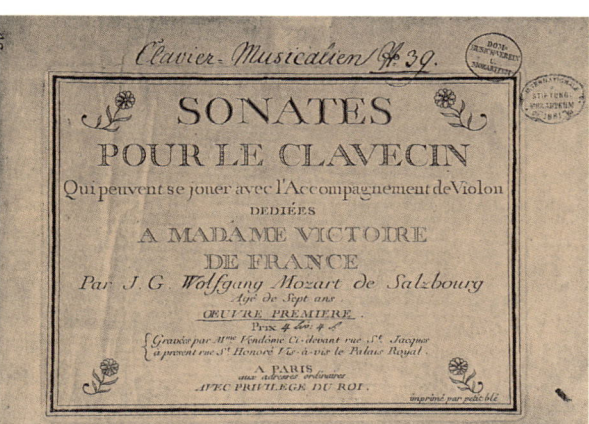

"He is a great humanist" wrote Leopold Mozart about Baron Friedrich Melchior von Grimm. Thanks to him 8-year-old Wolfgang's first piano sonatas were printed in Paris.

Emperor Joseph II was a keen supporter of the "National Singspiel", which encouraged Mozart as an opera composer. Painting by J. Hickell in the 2nd half of the 18th century.

Johann Christian Bach (1735–1782), youngest son of Johann Sebastian, was to have a lasting influence on Mozart

On the 24th July the Mozarts leave London after fifteen months and travel via Canterbury, Dover and Calais to Lille, where both father and son suffer from tonsilitis and have to stay for four weeks. The next station is Den Haag, where first Nannerl, then Wolfgang, fall seriously ill with abdominal typhoid. Reconvalescence takes two months. In the meantime Emperor Franz I dies in Innsbruck (18th August) and Joseph II becomes Emperor.

THE GRAND TOUR OF EUROPE

Wherever the Mozarts appeared the local aristocracy flung their doors open wide. Above: Afternoon tea with Prince Louis-Francois de Conti in the Temple, the main seat of the Order of the Knights Templar in Paris.

1766 Once recovered the children give concerts at the court in The Hague and then in Amsterdam, Utrecht and Antwerp. Whilst still in Holland Wolfgang publishes six *sonatas for piano and violin* (K 26–31) and presents them to Princess Caroline von Nassau-Weilburg.

On the 10th May they arrive in Paris, where they stay till mid-July, with a short three day intermezzo in Versailles in between. Then after Dijon, where the young boy sings a self-composed aria for the first time, it is on to Lyon then Lausanne, Berne, Zurich, Schaffhausen, Donaueschingen, Ulm and Augsburg to Munich.

On November the 9th Wolfgang plays for Elector Maximilian III Joseph again. Next day he suffers another attack of rheumatic fever that keeps him in bed for ten days. After one more concert at court, the Mozarts return to their home town on the Salzach river on the 29th of November. They are not quite

THE GRAND TOUR OF EUROPE 16

brimming with health but certainly with guilders and ducats. Wolfgang now speaks fluent French, English and Italian, besides German, and he has acquired the self-confidence of a well-travelled person, having been terribly flattered by Europe's high-ranking aristocrats, and he begins to sense that for him the circumstances in Salzburg will soon be restricting and limited and his genius will be hindered.

1767 For the usual performance of religious plays in Lent Mozart sets the first act of the German oratorio *Die Schuldigkeit des ersten Gebots* by Ignaz Anton von Weiser to music, (the second and third acts are delivered by Michael Haydn and Anton Cajetan Adlgasser respectively). After the performance in the Hall of Knights on the 12th of March, he receives a gold medal.

On the 15th of May in the University's Main Hall Wolfgang's earliest stage piece is performed, the Latin school opera *Apollo et Hyacinthus*. It is a commissioned piece for the annual end of term so-called final comedy and consists of ten music numbers based on the texts from Ovids "Metamorphoses" much like the principal of the Italian opera.

Throughout the summer the little fellow, just eleven years of age, composes symphonies, church sonatas and piano concertos as if they flowed from his pen on their own.

On the 11th of September, after just ten months' rest, the very career-minded father sets off once again with his children. This time to Vienna. But the family has to flee to Bohemia in October due to an outbreak of small-pox. Of course the children are already infected. During reconvalescence from the almost fatal illness, that robbed Wolfgang of his eye-sight for nine days and left him with pock marks on his face, he learns fencing in Olmütz.

1768 On the 10th of January, after two weeks of recuperation in Brünn, the Mozarts travel back to Vienna, where they are to stay for one whole year. Quarters are taken in the house named "Zum roten Säbel" (The Red Sable) (today: Wipplingerstraße 19).

In 1762 Archduke Joseph introduces young Mozart to his mother, Empress Maria Theresia. Wood carving from an original painting by Eduard Ender, c. 1870.

Franz Anton Mesmer (1734–1815), physician, close friend of the Mozarts and discoverer of "animal magnetism", which is heartily parodied in *Così fan tutte*.

After just nine days there is the first reception with Maria Theresia and Joseph II, followed shortly after by a second when one of the three *symphonies (K 43, 45* and probably *76)* were performed, that were said to be a result of the stay in Olmütz and the second stay in Vienna. In late winter the twelve-year-old begins work on his first Italian opera, *La finta semplice*, that the emperor personally encourages him to write. In July the work is finished. It adheres to the tradition of the Commedia dell'arte and consists of three acts and a total of 26 arias. The planned performance at first falls victim to intrigues.

Instead the Mozarts make the acquaintance of the physician, Franz Anton Mesmer, famous for his magnetic therapy. In his splendid house in the Rauchfangkehrergasse (today: Rasumofskygasse) the musical comedy *Bastien and Bastienne* was performed for the first time. The story, – the love between two poor peasant children is disturbed by a squire and then restored with the help of a soothsayer –, is set in a bucolic-naive environment, but the contents are nevertheless of revolutionary essence.

On the 7th of December, in the presence of the imperial family, Wolfgang conducts his *C minor Mass, K 139*, better known as the *Waisenhausmesse*, for the consecration of the new Waisenhaus church in the suburb of Landstrasse (today: Rennweg 91) "with greatest accuracy", as the "Wiener Diarium" commendably remarks. The trumpet concert, that is also performed for the first time at the same event, is later lost. Shortly before New Year, the Mozarts take their leave and after stops at the Abbeys of Melk and Lambach, they arrive in Salzburg on the 5th of January.

1769 During the eleven month rest back at home the musical fountain does not cease to bubble: already in February, the first performance of the *Missa brevis in D minor (K 65)* is heard in the Kollegienkirche. During carneval no less than 34 *menuets* are

A fanfare for Empress and Emperor: It was in their presence that the 13-year-old Mozart performed his *trumpet concert* and *Mass in C minor (K 139)*, for the first time, in the Waisenhaus Kirche (Orphanage Church) on the 7th of December 1768.

This painting, from 1770, by Saverio dalla Rosa shows Mozart at the age of about twelve. He has already travelled across half the Continent and made personal acquaintance with most of the rulers in half Europe.

produced. On the 1st of May in the Residenz Theatre, for the Archbishops name-day, *La finta semplice* is performed. In the summer months the new *serenades in D major (K 100)* and *G major (K 63)* are performed at the university. And in mid-October, in the abbey church of St. Peter's there is the first performance of the main religious work of this period: the *Dominicus Mass (K 66),* written for the first Mass of Wolfgang's childhood friend Rupert Hagenauer, who now becomes known as Pater Domenicus. This is his boyhood friend, who he shed tears for, when he became a monk.

At the end of November Wolfgang is appointed 3rd leader of the court orchestra. About the same time, in the introduction of the second issue of his "Violinschule", Leopold announces that he is going to write his son's biography – a plan that was never realized but one which left the world with the rich collection

SALZBURG

of the genius's letters, notebooks, early works and other documents. Mid-December father and son leave for Italy, armed with valuable references and a stately sum of 120 ducats as a subsidy from the Archbishop. "Now the German lout ceases to be and the Italian lout begins" he writes cheekily to his sister Nannerl, who has to stay at home this time. From now on he will call himself "Amadeo". The times of the child prodigy are over. The main reason for this first study trip to the promised land of music that will take fifteen months, is, besides the concert activities, to make contact with the world of contemporary opera and belcanto, the famous prima-donnas, castratis and impresarios, and also with composers and patrons of art.

1770 The first stop on the other side of the Brenner Pass is Verona, where the two Salzburgers get their first impressions of Italian enthusiasm in the easy-going atmosphere of Carneval. Impressive proof: the

The Governor General of Lombardy, Karl Count von Firmian, supported the Mozarts generously during their Italian travels. Engraving by Jacob Frey, 1781.

THE ITALIAN JOURNEY

The title-page of the first text book for the opera "Mitridates, Re di Ponto" which Mozart composed for Milan in 1770.

Father Giambattista Maritini

picture of the ingenious young boy painted by Saverio dalla Rosa for the music lover Pietro Lugiati. In Milan the Mozarts meet the Governor General of Lombardy (pertaining to Austria), Karl Joseph Count Firmian, whose diplomatic assistance helps clear the path for their further travels. They also become acquainted with Giovanni Battista Sammartini, the pioneer of early classic style in Italy, and Niccolò Piccinni, one of the main representatives of the opera buffa. Wolfgang receives his first commission from

THE ITALIAN JOURNEY 22

the Teatro Regio Ducal for the coming Carneval-Stagione. The order for a composition based on a tragedy from Racine: Dramma per musica *Mitridate, Re di Ponto*. In Bologna Mozart has a memorable meeting with the leading music theorist Giovanni Battista Martini and also with the legendary castrati Farinelli.

In Florence Mozart performs for the Grand Duke of Tuscany, the future Emperor Leopold II. In Rom, in the Sixtine Chapel he hears the Gregorio Allegris "Miserere" and then allegedly writes it down from memory, and here Pope Clemens XIV awards Mozart the Order of the Golden Spur First Class. In late summer, after a five-week stay in Naples, Mozart and his father having just recovered from the injuries caused by a carriage accident, take up quarters near Bologna in the country villa of Field-marshall Palavicini. Mozart is given composition tuition by Father Martini in the Accademia Filarmonica, at the end of which he is awarded the diploma that puts him among the honourable "Magistros Compositores".

After a period of intensive composing – "My fingers", he complains to his mother in a letter "are so sore from so much recitative writing" – he leads the first performance of *Mitridate* on the 26th of December in Milan to an overwhelming success.

Wolfgang Amadeus in the late-summer of 1777 wearing the "Order of the Golden Spur" (painting dates 1777), that was bestowed upon him by Pope Clemens XIV (below) in Rome.

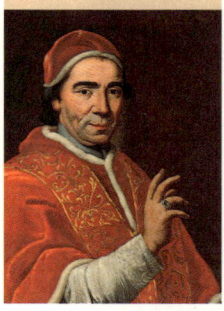

The Bay of Naples – in the southern-most city of their Italian journey Leopold and Wolfgang Amadeus Mozart stayed for a total of five weeks. Engraving by Anton Cardon, 1765.

THE ITALIAN JOURNEY

1771 On the 5th of January Wolfgang is appointed honorary 'Kapellmeister' of the Accademia Filarmonica of Verona. Mid-March, after stops in Turin, Milan and Venice on to Padua, Verona and Innsbruck, he is back home on the 28th of March. In his pocket he has two contracts: the opera for the Milanese carneval season 1772/73 *Lucio Silla,* and the two act *Ascanio in Alba* for the wedding festivities of the Archduke Ferdinand and Princess Beatrice d'Este of Modena.

Since 1765 the head of the family has been considering moving to a roomier apartment, but due to all the frequent travelling has always had to postpone the idea. Now that Mozart shows signs of oncoming puberty, his father takes the matter more seriously: "It has occured to me", he writes to his wife on the 20th of February from Venice, "that we cannot carry on sleeping like soldiers at home, Wolfgang is no longer 7 years-old etc." Nevertheless it will still be two years before the move is actually made.

During the summer many religious works and symphonies are written, among them a *Regina coeli (K 108),* the *Lauretan Litanei (K 109),* and, based

This decree, from the "Accademia Filarmonica" in Bologna, confirms that Mozart has been admitted to the ranks of "Magistros Compositores".

THE ITALIAN JOURNEY

The Canale Grande in Venice as Mozart saw it, during his stay. Engraving by M. Marieschi, 2nd half of the 18th century. Opposite page: Text book for the first performance of *Lucio Silla* (1773).

on a text by Metastasio, the oratorio *La Betulia liberata (K 118)*. A second, shorter trip to Italy (mid-August to mid-December) reaches it's climax with the first performance in Milan of *Ascanio in Alba*. Archduke Ferdinand is so enthusiastic about the "Azione teatrale" that he wants to employ Wolfgang, but is put off by a letter from his mother, the Empress, in which she argues that she does not think her son has need of "any composer or useless persons".

1772 Hieronymus Count Colloredo succeeds Siegmund Christoph Count Schrattenbach, who died in December of the previous year, as Prince Archbishop of Salzburg. For the occasion of his inthronisation at the end of April, W.A. Mozart completes the Serenata dramatica *Il sogno di Scipione*, which is performed for the first time in the ‚Residenz' at the beginning of May.

The months before and after are spent composing among other works eight *symphonies (K 96, 112, 128–130, 132–134)*, four *divertimenti (K 131, 136–138)*, six *menuets (K 164)*, some *songs, litanies, trio sonatas* and with the *O heiliges Band (K 148)* probably his first masonic song. In late August Colloredo appoints Mozart as leader of the court orchestra and pays him an annual salary of 150 guilders.

At the end of October father and son travel south a third time.

Mozart's employers – Archbishops Siegmund Christoph Count Schrattenbach (1753–72; below: engraving by Joh. Baptist Klauber, c. 1780) and Hieronymus Count Colloredo (1772–1803; above; painting by Xaver König, c. 1773).

FIRST MAJOR COMPOSITIONS

LUCIO SILLA

DRAMMA PER MUSICA

DA RAPPRESENTARSI

NEL REGIO-DUCAL TEATRO
DI MILANO

Nel Carnovale dell' anno 1773.

DEDICATO

ALLE LL. AA. RR.
IL SERENISSIMO ARCIDUCA

FERDINANDO

Principe Reale d' Ungheria, e Boemia, Arciduca d' Auſtria, Duca di Borgogna, e di Lorena ec., Ceſareo Reale Luogo-Tenente, Governatore, e Capitano Generale nella Lombardia Auſtriaca,

E LA

SERENISSIMA ARCIDUCHESSA

MARIA RICCIARDA BEATRICE D'ESTE

PRINCIPESSA DI MODENA.

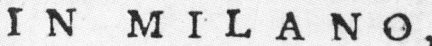

IN MILANO,

Preſſo Gio. Batiſta Bianchi Regio Stampatore
Con licenza de' Superiori.

Their destination is once again Milan, where *Lucia Silla* has to be rehearsed. The first performance on the 26th December in the Teatro Regio Ducal is to take place under rather difficult circumstances as the start is delayed because the Archduke arrives three hours after the audience. And although the piece is to be staged twenty-six times in a row in front of a full house, it is to be the last opera that he writes for Italy, the country, as he, later nostalgically, admits, in which "like no other ... was received with honours ... and respected".

1773 On the 17th of January the solo motette *Exsultate, jubilate* is performed for the first time in the Theatine church in Milan.

Mid-March Wolfgang Amadeus and his father are back home. In July the couple are given the Archbishop's consent to travel to Vienna once again, and on the 5th of August they are invited, probably to Laxenburg, to an audience with the Empress. Wolfgang's wish to be given employment at court is not fulfilled. In autumn, after their return journey home, the Mozarts at last move to their new abode on the Hannibalplatz (today: Makartplatz) and can escape the medieval confines of the old city on the left bank of the Salzach.

1774 During a short, uneventful phase of his life, but an all the more productive period as far as compositions are concerned, he composes, among other works, four *symphonies (K 182, 183, 201, 202)*, sixteen *menuets (K 176)*, the *Quintet (K 174)*, the first Mozart *piano concerto in D major (K 175)* and the *Missa brevis (K 194)* were produced. The climax in April is the first staging of two choir pieces from the opera Thamos, King in Egypt, in the Kärntnertortheater in Vienna. At last in autumn Wolfgang receives the commision for a new opera (in the mean time Christoph Willibald Gluck has been appointed Imperial and Royal Court Musician, with an annual salary of 2000 guilders). The court musical and theatre director in Munich has the wish for an opera buffa for the coming Carneval season. It's name: *La finta giardiniera*. The librettist: Gluck's text writer

Mozart's Violin (Mittenwald, first half of the 18th century) – He was accustomed to playing the violin. Nevertheless, it was the piano he was to master as a virtuoso.

Raniero de Calzabigi. At the beginning of December father and son travel to Munich. The premier performance is arranged for the 29th, but actually takes place, in the presence of the Elector Maximilian III, on the 13th of January 1775 in the Salvator theatre.

1775 Before setting off on the return journey to Salzburg amidst the merry-making of carneval there is still time to write and perform the so-called *Spatzen Mass (K 220)* and the offertorium motet *Miserecordias Domini (K 222)*. Back at home Mozart hurriedly composes the festival opera *Il Re pastore*. This work contains an overture and fourteen songs and is based on an old libretto adapted by the court chaplain Giambatista Varesco from Pietro Metastasio, whose texts have, at this point in time, been put to music over eight hundred times by different composers, and who is appointed "poet cesareo" in Vienna in 1730. On the 23rd of April the story about the noble-hearted Alexander the Great and the shepherd Aminta is staged for the first time at the Salzburg court theatre, for the occasion of the visit of Archduke Maximilian Franz, the youngest son of Maria Theresia.

Around this time Leopold Mozart's composing activities begin to ebb for ever.

The librettist Pietro Metastasio. Copper engraving by Mansfeld Sen., 1776. Below: Archduke Maximilian Franz. Copper engraving, c. 1760.

1776 About half way through the year Mozart's situation in his home town is becoming unbearable for him. The relationship with Archbishop Colloredo, his master and employer, who keeps him on a tight feudal leading rein, cools rapidly. But this does not keep the resentful subject from composing, within a few months and with enormous verve, a great number of *piano-* and *violin concertos, church sonatas, serenades* and *divertimenti*. On the 3rd of January the now much extended opera *Thamos, King of Egypt* is staged. Late in March the *Litaniae de venerabili altaris sacramento (K 243)*, mid-June the first *Lodron Nachtmusik (Divertimento in F major, K 247)*, and one month later, on the occasion of Elizabeth Haffner's wedding, the *Haffner serenade (K 250)*. The twenty-year-old has now completed about 300 works.

1777 In March, the Mozarts again ask their Prince for permission to take leave, to enable them to make another trip but he refuses. Upon which Mozart hands in his notice. This is accepted and he sets off with his mother in mid-September, with the prospect in mind of finding an adequate position at a court in Germany. First stops are made in Munich and Augsburg, where not even a foot in the door helps. "In the name of God! Patience!" warns the father from home. "There is just no chance here with the Elector", Mozart writes back straight away, leaving no hope whatsoever, but raving on about his amiable cousin Maria Anna Thekla: "We two are just right together, because she is quite naughty too. We are teasing people together, which is real fun."

Under the rule of Elector Palatinate Karl Theodor, Mannheim became a centre of cultural activities, second to none. However, although the Elector was inclined to favour Mozart, there was no appointment for him at court. Painting by Joh. Georg Ziesenis, c. 1770

Of more importance are the acquaintances that Wolfgang Amadeus, now calling himself Amadé, makes in Mannheim, the "paradise of artists" (F. H. Jacobi), where one can "swim in the lust of music" (F. G. Klopstock). Although he tries, unsuccessfully, for a post at the court of the aesthetic Elector Karl Theodor, his friendships with many of the famous court musicians prove to be of valuable inspiration. Especially "Kapellmeister" Christian Cannabich, for whose daughter he writes the *piano sonata in C major (K 309/284b)*. The meeting with the musician family Weber, the family that one generation later the world famous composer Carl Maria (the "Golden Bullet" and "Oberon") is born into, proves fateful. Mozart falls madly in love with Aloisia, the second eldest of

Mannheim was chosen by those musical pioneers whose compositions gave rise to the Viennese Classical Style, which developed while Mozart was young. Engraving, 2nd half of the 18th century.

A Silhouette, from c. 1777, of Aloisia Weber (1760–1830), who Mozart worshipped for a long time. Below: A portrait of the Mozart family by Johann Nepomuk Della Croce, completed in winter 1780/81.

the four daughters, who is a highly talented singer. She is the reason that the sojourn for mother and son in Mannheim lasts nearly five months in spite of letters from the father urging their return.

1778 After a trip to the court of Princess Caroline von Nassau-Weilburg in Kirchheimbolanden, with the Webers but without mother, where Mozart and Aloisia perform together, Leopold shows his authority. Mother and son continue at last to Paris. On the 23rd of March they arrive in the Seine Metropole. At this time the dispute between the followers of Gluck and the followers of Piccinni (that is to say the supporters of the court oriented French lyrical tragedy against those of the Italian buffa) is reaching its climax. There is no great success for Mozart here. "If this were a place", he writes, unflatteringly, "where the people had ears, a heart to feel and just a little understanding for music and a little taste, well I would laugh with all my heart. But I am surrounded

THROUGH GERMANY TO FRANCE

The immortal "Bäsle", alias Maria Anna Thekla Mozart, from Augsburg was the recipient of Mozart's rude-witty and erotic letters. Pencil drawing c. 1777/78.

by beasts and creatures (as far as music is concerned)." At least he is given one small commission for a composition. On the 11th of June the Ballett Pantomime *Les petit riens* by Jean-Georges Noverres is performed for the first time in the Opéra, partly with Mozart's music. Almost straight after his *Paris symphony in D major (K 297)* is performed in the Swiss hall in the Tuileries, at the "concert spirituel". But then his mother becomes ill (24th June) and dies (3rd July). At the end of September he leaves the city that left him without any perspectives. Mozart, thus disillusioned and burdened with debts, sets off in the direction of Germany.

After staying in Strasbourg, Mannheim and at the abbey of Kaisheim near Donauwörth, Mozart reaches Munich for Christmas.

1779 After his proposal of marriage was turned down by Aloisia, who had found an engagement as a singer in Munich, he returned, probably in the company of his loyal cousin Bäsle, to the city on the Salzach. Mid-January he joins the Archbishop's troop once again. For 450 guilders he becomes the court organist. Now a period of permanent composing begins. One master-piece after another is created – for the

This painting from c. 1780 shows Joseph Lange (1751–1831), actor and husband of Aloisia Weber. He was the author of the famous unfinished portrait of Mozart.

Aloisia Lange, née Weber (1760–1839), was Mozart's childhood love and preferred singer.

church: *vespers, choral works* and the *coronation Mass in C major (K 317)*, for profane customers: the *concert for two horns (K 334)*, further *marches, menuets*, the *symphony in B major (K 319)* and the *Sinfonia concertante in E flat major (K 364)* and also the musical comedy *Zaide* which, as far as one knows today, was not to be performed until 1866.

In the mean time the Weber family has moved from Munich to Vienna, where the father, Fridolin, dies on the 23rd of October.

1780 The amount of work this year is the same as the previous one. Mozart enriches his œuvre with a *Mass in C major (K 337)*, a *symphony in C major (K 338)* as well as some more *vespers, sonatas* and *menuets*.

In September the Mozarts meet Emanuel Schikaneder, who has come to Salzburg with his troop of actors, singers and dancers for the winter season. They get to know him better playing skittles and shooting.

In October Aloisia marries the actor and painter Joseph Lange. In the meantime Mozart has received a commission from Munich to write the carneval-seria for 1781. The text from the sagas of Troy about the

SALZBURG

return of the King of Crete, Idomeneo, and the amorous entanglements of his son Idamante and the daughters of Priamos and Agamemnon, Ilia and Elettra, is produced by the Salzburg resident Court Chaplain Giambattista Varesco. On the 5th of November Mozart makes his way to the Bavarian residence, to complete the score with the actors (in those days a usual occurance) and to begin with rehearsals. On the 29th of the month Maria Theresia dies in Vienna. Successor is her son Joseph II.

The death of Maria Theresia in 1780. Her son and patron of Mozart, Joseph II, begins as Emperor with the "Revolution from above". Soon the desire to return to the moderate reforms of his mother is widespread. Silhouette by Hieronymus Löschenkohl.

1781 On the 29th of January, two days after his birthday, Mozart leads the premier performance of the three act "Dramma per musica" *Idomeneo, Re di Creta*. Leopold and Nannerl are present and afterwards the family enjoy the carnival in Munich to their heart's content. Mid-March, during a visit to his relatives in Augsburg, he receives an order from Archbishop Colloredo, who is already in Vienna, to follow him to the Imperial City. In spite of the obligation, he writes later "I looked forward to Vienna without knowing why." As if he knows that the city on the Danube will become his home for the rest of his life?

The title-page of Johann Wenzel Schmid's piano score of the opera *Idomeneo*. Edited in Leipzig.

Having only just been a guest of the high ranking Bavarian aristocracy, a friend among friends of the most exquisite orchestra on the continent, he now finds himself once again on the same level as servants, cooks and grooms in the "Deutschordernshaus" (House of the Teutonic Knights) (Singerstraße 7), the Vienna residence of the Archbishop, where he is constantly and relentlessly controlled.

Then, when he is prevented from accepting any other form of employment, and, after he misses a concert for the Emperor because of duties elsewhere, the inevitable break comes. Mozart provokes his dismissal and is given the legendary send-off with a "kick in the pants out of the door", by the Archbishop's groom and chief caterer, Karl Joseph Count Arco.

Just after his arrival in March, Mozart had contacted the Weber family. And now the lady of the house, Maria Cäcilia Weber, was to allow him to stay on the second floor of her home on the corner of Milchgasse/Tuchlauben. It is here where Wolfgang and Constanze, the sister of the adored Aloisia, get to know each other a lot better! But this does not stop him from working eagerly on his career as a freelance composer, pianist and music teacher. Soon he appears not only at the concerts and soireés of the aristocracy, and in the salons of the bourgeois, but also at his very own, personally organized concerts, which in those days were arranged entirely at the composers and performers own risk. He is euphoric because of his success and makes a note about Vienna, that it is just perfect – "for my métier – the best place in the world".

At the end of July he receives the libretto for the *Abduction from the Seraglio* by Johann Gottlieb Stephanie. And just one month later the first act of the musical comedy is finished.

At the beginning of September Mozart moves from the Weber's house "because of people's gossip", to a room on the Graben. On the day before Christmas, the famous competition between him and the piano virtuoso Muzio Clementi is held in the Hofburg Palace.

Mozart's comtemporary, the very famous Italian pianist and composer, Muzio Clementi.

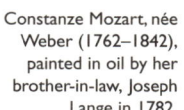

Constanze Mozart, née Weber (1762–1842), painted in oil by her brother-in-law, Joseph Lange in 1782.

35 THE ABDUCTION FROM THE SERAGLIO

1782   During spring, he spends most of his time working on the *Abduction,* and attempts to gain his father's consent – at first without success – for the proposed marriage to Constanze. At the end of May the series of concerts begins in the Augarten. On the 16th July he conducts the *Abduction from the Seraglio* in the Burgtheater.

1783   Yet another year of concert activity. Especially his cooperation in many Burgtheater concerts is highly commended by Maestro Gluck and the Emperor. Around this time Mozart meets the man who is to play an enormously important role in his future opera works, the libretto writer Lorenzo Da Ponte.

After yet another two changes of address, – first the Kohlmarkt, then the Judenplatz, – Mozart is to become a father for the first time. Little Raimund Leopold doesn't live very long though, after just two months, he dies of abdominal typhoid. Late in July Mozart and Constanze pay his father in Salzburg the long awaited visit. There he works on an opera buffa, *Lo sposo deluso ossia La rivalità di tre donne per un solo amante.* And parallelly he begins work on the "opera book" by Varesco, the *Goose from Cairo,* of which only fragments are produced, probably because the text is so poor. On the 26th of October the C minor Mass (K 427) is performed in St. Peter's, and the day after, the return journey to Vienna is made.

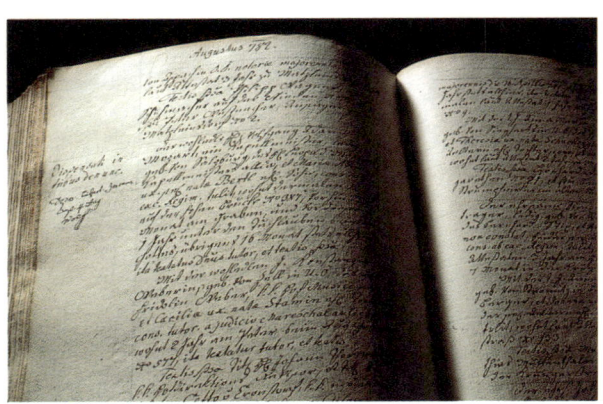

Written proof of Mozart's marriage to Constanze, on the 4th August, 1782 in St. Stephan's Cathedral.

WEDDING

The title-page of the first piano score from the *Abduction*. It was published by Abbé Starck without the composer's knowledge.

Mozart is not to know it, but he is saying goodbye to his home town forever. In Linz a break in the journey home is made and for three weeks he stays at the home of Count Thun-Hohenstein. He makes a note just before a concert in the local theatre: "As I don't have a symphony with me, I am going to write a new one, head over heels." The result, the *Linzer symphony (K 425)*, is to be heard on the 4th of November for the first time.

1784 At the start of the year, another change of address. The new home: Trattnerhof on the Graben. In the month of February, Mozart, who is permanently composing, begins to make an "Index of all my works" (which future generations are to find of considerable help when sorting out his œuvre). At the private concerts of patrons like Prince Golycin or Counts Esterházy, Zichy and Pálffy, he plays the piano and conducts. At the same time he enjoys great success (also financially) at his numerous subscription concerts. His audience now includes not only members of the high ranking aristocracy, but also the low-ranking and moneyed aristocracy and the middle class.

At this time, as letters offer proof, he meets with two of Italy's main representatives of the opera buffa, the Maestri Giovanni Paisiello and Guiseppe Sarti.

Two of Mozart's influential companions: Christoph Willibald Gluck (1714–1787; above) and the librettist, Lorenzo Da Ponte (1749–1838; below).

The cover of the index of Mozart's own works, which he began keeping in February of 1784.

Mozart's sister, Maria Anna alias "Nannerl". Painting c. 1785.

On the 23rd of August his sister Nannerl marries the lawyer and twice widower Johann Baptist Franz von Berchtold zu Sonnenburg in St. Gilgen. "Well, good gracious! it is indeed time for me to write to you, if this letter is to find you still a vestal! a couple of days later and – it's gone." This is how Mozart congratulates his sister, only to be inflicted on the very same day by a kidney seizure that confines him to his bed for a number of weeks. On the 21st of September his second son, Carl Thomas, is born (see 1858). Just a short while later the family moves to a much roomier, and comparatively luxurious abode – the "Figaro house" in the Domgasse, adapted as a museum today. On the 14th of December Mozart is initiated as an Entered Apprentice Freemason in the lodge "Zur Wohltätigkeit" (to charity), and three weeks later on the 7th of January he becomes a Fellow Craft.

1785 Joseph Haydn visits Mozart at his home and hears three of the *string quartets*, that are later to be dedicated to him. In the same year he congratulates the proud father Leopold at a personal meeting: "I say to you before God, as an honest man, your son is the greatest composer, that I know personally and by name: he has taste, and beyond that the greatest knowledge of composition." In February, in Leopold's presence, the first of Mozarts Friday concerts is performed in the "Flour Pit". The *piano concerto in d minor (K 466)* is given for the first time. In the Burgtheater, at one of the "musician's society" evenings in mid-March, the new oratorio *Davidde penitente*, that is based musically on the *Mass in c minor (K 427)*, is heard. On the 1st of September – Leopold is back home in Salzburg since April – the publishing house Artaria prints the *six string quartets* for Joseph Haydn, the *symphonies K 385, 319* and a number of *piano concertos*. A little later Mozart begins work on a new opera – *Le nozze di Figaro (The marriage of Figaro)*, the libretto from Lorenzo Da Ponte according to Beaumarchais. Also in this year two important masonic compositions are written – the cantata the *masonic joy (K 471)* and composed in remembrance of two deceased brothers the *masonic mourning music (K 477)*.

1786 The very talented seven-year-old Johann Nepomuk Hummel from Bratislava moves in with Mozart and receives tuition.

In honour of Duke Albert of Saxony and his wife Archduchess Marie Christine, Joseph II's sister, Mozart's musical comedy *Der Schauspieldirektor* is

Johann Baptist Franz von Berchtold zu Sonnenburg (1736–1801), Lawyer and husband of Nannerl Mozart.

Joseph Haydn (1732–1809) and Mozart were good friends, and also admirers of each other.

Pierre Augustin Caron de Beaumarchais

Johann Nepomuk Hummel lived in Mozart's home and was his pupil from 1786–88. Below: The Orangerie in Schönbrunn Palace. Copper engraving by Hieronymus Löschenkohl, 1785.

staged in the Orangerie in the Palace of Schönbrunn. The text is by Johann Gottlieb Stephanie Junior. The composer receives fifty ducats from the Emperor.

On the 1st of May the first performance of *Le nozze di Figaro* is staged in the Burgtheater with tremendous success. This is the opera-buffa with the disrespectful presentation of aristocratic customs, written by Pierre Augustin Caron de Beaumarchais, that had just been banned from the stages of France, England and Germany. The weeks just before, Mozart performed *Idomeneo*, privately, for Prince Auersperg and conducted his last concert in the Burgtheater.

On the 18th of October Mozart's third child, Johann Thomas Leopold, is born. Only to die of suffocation just four weeks later.

At an Advent concert in the Casino, the *piano concerto in C major K 503* is performed for the first time.

This is the culmination and end of the series of twelve such works, that Mozart created and presented – most of them personally – to his subscription audience over the last three years. Mozarts successful Vienna period nears its end. What is now to begin are years of economic worries.

On the 18th December in Eutin in Holstein Constanze's cousin, Carl Maria von Weber, is born.

LE NOZZE DI FIGARO 40

Ludwig van Beethoven (1770–1827; lithography by Josef Kriehuber, 1865). In April of 1787, Beethoven played in front of Mozart, probably with the intention of taking lessons – a never realized intent.

1787 Since the *Marriage of Figaro* was staged at the National Theatre in Prague about the beginning of December 1786, the Bohemian capital has experienced a Mozart-mania. The reason for this is not only musical but also political: the opposition of the German-Bohemian national theatre against the court-oriented Italian opera. In the first days of January the much acclaimed Maestro follows the call to Prague, where he receives a commission to compose an opera for the coming season. "Here nothing is spoken but – figaro; nothing is played, sung, whistled or blown but – figaro; no opera visited but – figaro and eternally figaro; certainly a great honour for me," he writes to his friend, Gottfried von Jacquin, in Vienna. Before returning to Vienna in mid-February, he presents the enraptured people of Prague with a personally conducted performance of *Figaro* and the new – although completed in Vienna, so-called *Prague – symphony in D major (K 504)*.

At the beginning of April Ludwig van Beethoven comes to Vienna, receives tuition from Mozart, but after only two weeks has to return home to Bonn for

Lorenzo Da Ponte (1749–1838), Mozart's congenial librettist.

personal reasons. Soon after that the Mozarts move to a cheaper home in the suburb of Landstraße.

On the 28th of May Leopold Mozart passes away at the age of 67 in Salzburg. He is buried in the Sebastian cemetery. On the 10th of August Mozart completes the *Kleine Nachtmusik (K 525)*.

In early October he once again travels to Prague with Da Ponte and the ensemble to rehearse *Don Giovanni*. According to legend Mozart composes the entire overture in just one night, and the next day, the 29th, the triumphal first performance of the dramma giocoso about the excessive libertine lover takes place

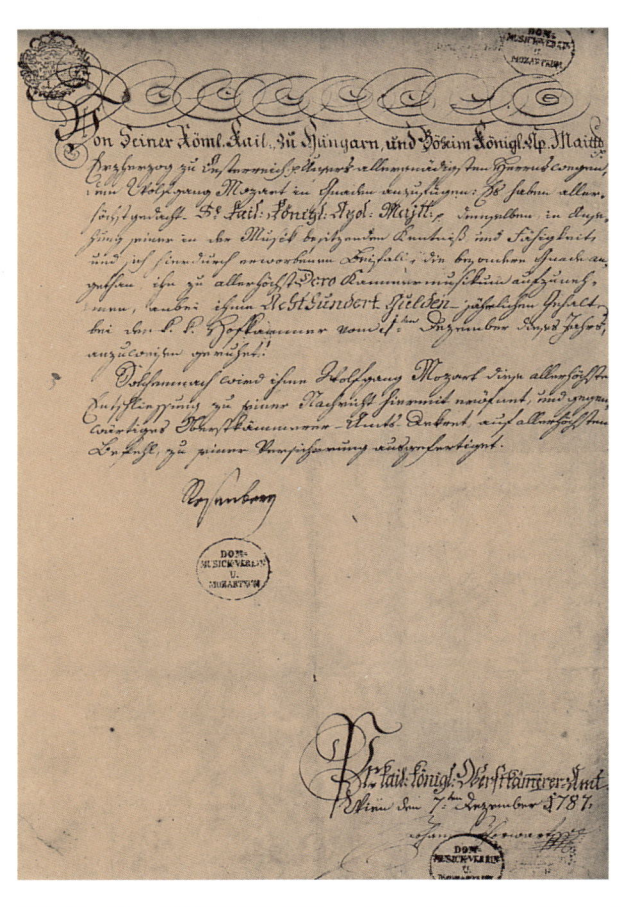

The decree in which Joseph II appoints Mozart as Court Chamber Musician. The date: 6th December, 1787. The salary: 800 guilders per annum.

PRAGUE SYMPHONY

in the Nostitz National Theatre. At the beginning of November he composes one of his most beautiful arias: *Bella mia fiamma (K 528)* for the singer and close friend Josepha Duschek in her villa Bertramka in the district of Smíchov in Prague.

Back in Vienna again, another change of address – back to the inner-city. On the 6th of December Mozart is appointed composer at court by Joseph II with an annual salary of 800 guilders "on account of his knowledge and versatility in music, which has earned him deserved applause". On the 15th Gluck dies, on the 27th Mozart is a father for the fourth time. Little Theresia only lives to the age of six months.

1788 The performance of the *Abduction* in the Kärntnertor Theatre brings the era of German musical comedies to a close for the time being. While Mozart composes mainly dances for the ball-season (apart from the *piano concerto in D major,* the *Coronation concerto (K 537)*, his financial situation becomes precarious. What follows is a change of address. Mozart moves to a cheaper suburban home.

From now on he has to borrow money from his friend and Fellow Mason Michael Puchberg. And in addition symptoms which show that his health is beginning to suffer become evident. Even though the Emperor is to call it "heavenly", the first performance of *Don Giovanni* on the 7th May is only relatively successful. Nevertheless it is repeated fourteen times till the end of the year. Over the summer he writes his last three *symphonies,* the *E-flat major, G major* and the *Jupiter in C major (K 543, 550* and *551)*. Mozart's star as an independent concert organizer is beginning to fade.

1789 Another change of abode at the beginning of the year. Early April in the company of his Fellow Brother, Prince Karl Lichnowsky, Mozart travels northwards through Prague to Germany. In Prague he receives a commission for a new opera from a theatre-entrepreneur called Guardasoni, but this turns out to be a dubious order. In Dresden Mozart plays his *coronation concert* for Elector Friedrich August III,

An aquarelle by J. Quaglio, showing the earliest, still existing, scene-picture from a Don Giovanni performance – the church-yard scene. Painted in 1789 in Mannheim.

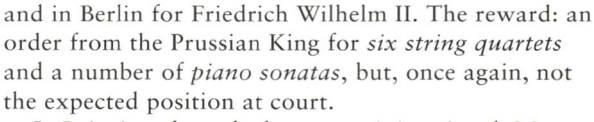

and in Berlin for Friedrich Wilhelm II. The reward: an order from the Prussian King for *six string quartets* and a number of *piano sonatas*, but, once again, not the expected position at court.

In Leipzig, where the last portrait is painted, Mozart hears one of his motets in the Thomas school, where Johann Sebastian Bach was cantor, and reacts overjoyed: "Now that really is something one can learn a lot from!"

In July, a month after his return, Constanze becomes ill and goes to the Spa town of Baden for the first time for health reasons. Mid-November her fifth child is born but dies almost immediately after birth. Mozart spends the rest of the year composing the music for a new opera buffa, the work in two-acts is *Così fan tutte (K 588)*. On New Year's Eve, which is spent at home in the company of Haydn and Puchberg, Mozart holds a first rehearsal.

1790 January the 26th sees the very successful first performance of the new opera in the Vienna Burgtheater. It is a partly cynical, partly funny story about Ferrando and Guglielmo who want to put their fiancées to the test by each trying (successfully) to seduce the other's betrothed. The libretto is once again from the pen of Da Ponte. On the 20th of February Joseph II. dies. Mozart's ever increasing

Mozart's Freemason brother and travel companion, Prince Karl Lichnowsky.

depts threaten to cripple his creativity. Especially since his expectations of being given the post of second "Kapellmeister" by the new Emperor, Leopold II, remain unfulfilled.

In the early summer Constanze is again not too well and spends time in Baden at the Spa. At the end of September Mozart sets off in high spirits to Leopold's coronation. But during the festivities there he is ignored. Some consolation is found, however, on the return journey, when he performs in Mainz at the palace of the Elector, and in Mannheim he sees the first performance of his *Figaro* in Germany. During Mozart's absence, Constanze has meanwhile moved to the Rauhensteingasse, their last joint residence.

Coronation ceremony for Emperor Leopold II in the Bartholomäus Church in Frankfurt.

1791 Shortly after New Year Mozart ends his *piano concerto in B major (K 595)*. This performance on the 4th of March in the "Jahn hall", at which he plays the piece for the first time, is to be his last public appearance in concert.

In early May he is given the appointment of unsalaried assistant to the "Kapellmeister" of St. Stephan's. In the same month he begins work on the masonic opera *The Magic Flute*. Emanuel Schikaneder is the one who commissions it. It is staged for the first time on the 30th of September in his Freihaus-Theatre in

The announcement of the forthcoming first performance of Così fan tutte in the old Vienna Burgtheater on the 26th of January 1790.

COSÌ FAN TUTTE

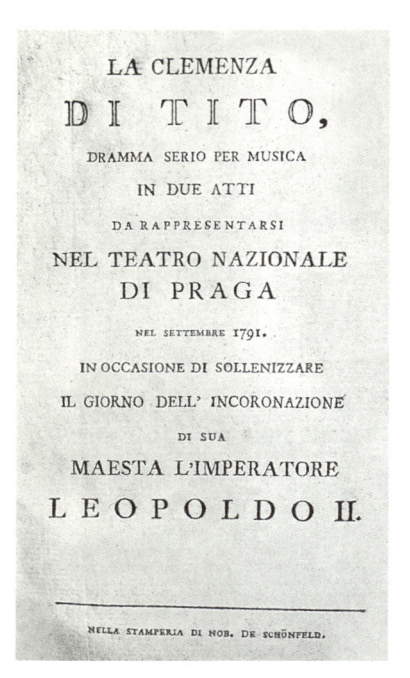

La clemenza di Tito (K 621): title-page of the libretto, Prague 1791.
Above right: Piano score for the *Requiem*, completed by Franz Xaver Süßmayr.

Mozart's two sons: Carl Thomas and Franz Xaver Wolfgang. By Hans Hansen, c. 1798.

the suburb of Wieden, and the first performance is conducted by Mozart himself. Because of its enormous success, the opera is repeated twenty times already just in the following month.

At the beginning of June Constanze goes to Baden for health reasons. On the 26th her last son, Franz Xaver Wolfgang, is born (see 1844). During one of the frequent visits Mozart pays his wife in Baden, he writes the *Ave Verum (K 618)*.

In July an anonymous courier, later to become death's messenger in romantic biographers' eyes, orders a *Requiem* for a Lodge Brother Franz Count Walsegg-Stuppach, which is to be composed in memory of his deceased young wife. Also in July, he receives an order for a coronation opera from the Bohemian Estates in Prague. Already at the end of August he leaves for Prague for the third time with the almost completed opera, with his wife and his composition-pupil Franz Xaver Süßmayr, who after

THE MAGIC FLUTE
46

Mozart's death finished both the *Requiem* and the *horn concert in D major (K 412* and *514)*. After a festival performance of *Don Giovanni* on the 2nd September, *La clemenza di Tito*, an opera seria in two acts, with a libretto from Caterino Mazzolà, is performed for the first time in the National Theatre. In the audience: the recently crowned King of Bohemia, Leopold II.

On the 15th of November, completely overworked and depressed, (at this point in time he is convinced that he is being continuously shadowed and poisoned), Mozart finishes the *Kleine Freimaurerkantate (K 623)*, which is performed three days later at the opening ceremony of the new lodge-temple. On the 20th of November he has to take to his bed. On the 4th of December, suffering from nausea, spasms and swollen joints, he gives Süßmayr instructions on how to finish the *Requiem,* and even has a rehearsal held.

On the 5th of December shortly before one a.m. his life is over. He finds his last place of rest in an anonymous communal grave in the cemetery of St. Marx.

Franz Count Walsegg-Stuppach. Silhouette by Francois Gonord, 1786.

The death and funeral of the Maestro gave rise to legends in abundance. This coloured engraving "Convoi du Pauvre" belonged to Ludwig van Beethoven. He kept it as a symbolic reminder of Mozart.

REQUIEM AND DEATH

1798 The Czech teacher and music critic Franz Xaver Niemetschek publishes the first Mozart biography of any importance. In the same year the Leipzig publishing house, Breitkopf & Härtel, announces the attempt to publish Mozart's complete works – a daring editorial venture, that the firm does eventually succeed in doing in the years 1877–83 (with an appendix from 1910).

1828 In Leipzig the Mozart biography by Constanze's second husband, the deceased diplomat Georg Nikolaus Nissen, is published posthumously by the widow herself.

1829 Mozart's sister, Nannerl, dies in Salzburg on the 29th October. The English composer and publisher Vincent Novello on a pilgrimage to the places where his hero Wolfgang Amadeus had worked, had only just stopped at the sister's home in Salzburg to hand over a donation of money that had been collected amongst Mozart's admirers in London.

Georg Nikolaus Nissen (1761–1826), Constanze's second husband. Painting by Ferdinand Jagemann, 1809.

Title-page of the first edition of the "Complete Works" published in 1798, by Breitkopf & Härtel.

CONSTANZE'S DEATH 48

1841   Archbishop Friedrich zu Schwarzenberg establishes the "Dom-Musik-Verein" to revive the tradition of church music. Also "as an educational establishment for music" and as a memorial to the great son of the city the "Mozarteum".

1842   The unveiling of Ludwig von Schwanthaler's Mozart monument takes place in the presence of both sons in the early part of September in Salzburg. On the 6th of March, Mozart's widow Constanze dies.

1844   On the 29th July Franz Xaver Wolfgang Mozart dies in Karlsbad, the sixth (second surviving) child of Constanze and Wolfgang Amadeus. Already at the age of eleven, he had a piano quartet published – like father like son. Later he studied under Sigismund von Neukomm, J. G. Albrechtsberger and Antonio Salieri, and lived, from 1808 on, in Lemberg where he worked as a piano teacher, pianist and composer.

Concert tours took him through Russia, Poland, Austria, Germany, Denmark and Italy. As a composer the works he left behind included piano concertos, chamber- and piano music, choral works and Lieder. The legacy he left to the Dom-Musik-Verein and Mozarteum, contained numerous mementos including fragments of compositions by his father.

1858   On the 2nd of November Mozart's eldest son, Carl Thomas, dies. He had studied composition periodically, but in 1797 had already completed an apprenticeship as a tradesman in Livorno and then later finally became a civil servant in Milan.

1862   Ludwig Ritter von Köchels "Choronologisch-thematisches Verzeichnis sämmtlicher Tonwerke Wolfgang Amadé Mozart's" (Complete chronological-thematical Index of the musical works of W. A. M) appears in print, published by Breitkopf & Härtel. It covers 626 works, including 20 operas and music comedies, 41 symphonies, 32 concerts for one or more solo instruments and 41 concerts for one or more pianos.

Sebastian's Cemetery in Salzburg. The graves of Constanze and Leopold Mozart.

Mozart's youngest child, Franz Xaver Wolfgang (1791–1844)

Ludwig Ritter von Köchel (1800–1877). He was the author of the "Complete chronological-thematical Index of the musical works of W. A. Mozart".

SONE

```
Wolfgang Nikolaus Pertl
Salzburg 1667–1724
St. Gilgen
  ⚭
Eva Rosina Barbara Altmann
Stein/Donau 1681–1755
Salzburg
                            │
                            ├── Anna Maria Walpurga Pertl      ┌── Maria Anna Walburga
                            │   St. Gilgen 1720–1778 Paris     │   Ignatia Mozart
                            │     ⚭                            │   1751–1829
                            │   Johann Georg Leopold Mozart    │     ⚭
                            │   Augsburg 1719–1787 Salzburg ───┤   Joh. Bapt. Freih. Berchtold
                            │                                  │   zu Sonnenburg
                            │                                  └── 1736–1801

Johann Georg Mozart
Augsburg 1679–1736
  ⚭
Anna Maria Sulzer
Augsburg 1696–1766
                            │
                            ├── Franz Alois Mozart
                            │   Augsburg 1727–1791             ── Maria Anna Thekla Mozart
                            │     ⚭                               "Bäsle"
                            │   Maria Viktoria Eschenbach         Augsburg 1758–1841
                            │   1727–1808


                                                                  Josepha Weber
                                                                  1759–1819
                                                                    ⚭ 1. Franz Hofer 1755–1796
                                                                    ⚭ 2. Fr. S. Mayer 1773–1835

                            ┌── Fridolin Weber                     Aloisia Weber 1761–1839
                            │   Augsburg 1733–1779                   ⚭
                            │     ⚭                                 Joseph Lange 1751–1831
                            │   Maria Cäcilia Stamm
                            │   1727–1793                           Sophie Weber 1763–1846
                            │                                         ⚭
Fridolin Weber              │                                       J. Haibel 1762–1826
Zell am Wiesental 1691–1754 │
  ⚭                         │
Maria Eva Chelar            │
1698–1774                   │
                            │   Franz Anton Weber                  Carl Maria von Weber
                            └── Augsburg 1734–?                    Augsburg 1786–1826
                                  ⚭                                  ⚭
                                Genoveva Brenner                   Caroline Brandt
                                1764–1798                          1794–1852
```

GENEALOGICAL TREE OF THE MOZART, PERTL AND WEBER FAMILIES

Johann Chrysostomus
Wolfgang Theophilus (Amadeus) Mozart
Salzburg 27. 1. 1756–
5. 12. 1791 Vienna
∞
Maria Constanze
Cäcilia Josepha Johanna Aloisia Weber
Zell im Wiesental 5. 1. 1762–
6. 3. 1842 Salzburg

Raimund Leopold Mozart
1783

Carl Thomas Mozart
1784–1858

Johann Thomas Leopold Mozart
1786

Theresia Constanzia Adelheid
Friedericke Maria Anna Mozart
1787–1788

Anna Mozart
1789

Franz Xaver Mozart
1791–1844

Maria Caroline Friederika Auguste
von Weber 1818–1819

Max Maria Philipp von Weber
1822–1881

Alexander Heinrich Victor Maria
von Weber 1825–1844

MOZART'S JOURNEYS

To Munich (Jan./Feb. 1762)

To Vienna (Sept. 1762 till Jan. 1763)
Salzburg – Passau – Linz – Mauthausen – Stein – Vienna (on the 11th December, short trip to Bratislava) – Linz – Salzburg

Grand Tour of Europe (June 1763 till November 1766)
Salzburg – Munich – Augsburg – Ulm – Ludwigsburg – Schwetzingen – Mannheim – Frankfurt-on-Main – Bonn – Cologne – Aachen – Brussels – Paris/Versailles (November till April) – London (April 1764 till July 1765) – Ghent – Antwerp – The Hague/Amsterdam (September 1765 till March 1766) – Paris/Versailles (May till July 1766) – Dijôn – Lyons – Geneva – Lausanne – Zürich – Schaffhausen – Donaueschingen – Ulm – Biberach – Augsburg – Munich – Salzburg

To Vienna (September 1767 till January 1769)
Salzburg – Lambach – Linz – Melk – Vienna – (October 1767 till January 1768 side trip to Brno and Olomouc) – Salzburg

First journey to Italy (Dec. 1769 till March 1771)
Salzburg – Innsbruck – Verona – Milan – Modena – Bologna – Florence – Viterbo – Rome – Naples – Rome – Loretto – Imola – Bologna (July till Oct.) – Milan – Turin (Oct. till Dec.) – Verona – Venice – Vicenza – Brescia – Innsbruck – Salzburg

Second journey to Italy (Aug. till Dec. 1771)
Salzburg – Verona – Milan – Verona – Salzburg

Third journey to Italy (Oct. 1772 till March 1773)
Salzburg – Milan and back

To Vienna (July till Sept. 1773)
To Munich (Dec. 1774 till March 1775)

To Paris (Sept. 1777 till Jan. 1779)
Salzburg – Munich – Augsburg – Mannheim (Oct. till March) – Paris (March till Sept.) – Strasbourg – Mannheim (Nov./Dec.) – Munich – Salzburg

To Munich and Vienna
(Nov. 1780/March 1781 …)

From Vienna to Salzburg (July till Oct. 1783)

First journey to Prague (Jan./Feb. 1787)
Vienna – Prague – Vienna

Second journey to Prague (Oct./Nov. 1787)
Vienna – Prague – Vienna

To Berlin (April till June 1789)
Vienna – Prague – Dresden – Leipzig – Potsdam – Berlin – Prague – Vienna

To Frankfurt-on-Main (Sept. till Nov. 1790)
Vienna – Regensburg – Nürnberg – Aschaffenburg – Frankfurt – Mainz – Mannheim – Ulm – Augsburg – Munich – Vienna

Third journey to Prague (Aug./Sept. 1791)
Vienna – Prague – Vienna

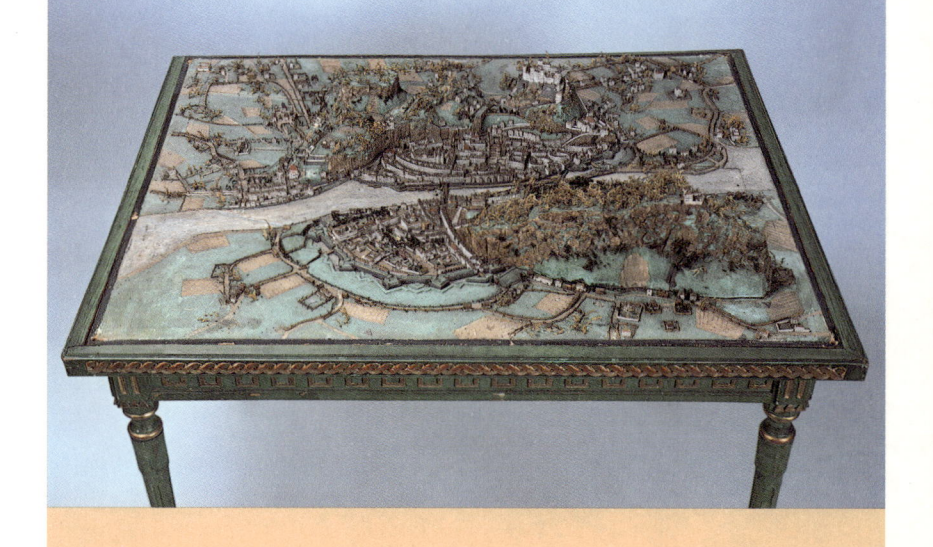

SALZBURG

Mozart's birthplace in the Getreidegasse 9, in Salzburg. Painting from the early 19th century, artist unknown.

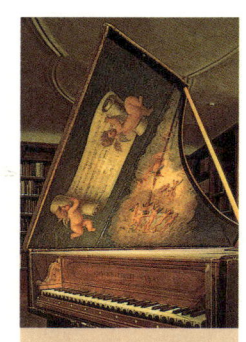

17th century Venetian cembalo on exhibit in Mozart's place of birth.

1 Mozart's Birthplace

(Getreidegasse 9 = Universitätsplatz 14): Joannes Chrysostomus Wolfgangus Theophilus alias Wolfgang Amadeus Mozart came into the world on the 27th of January 1756 at eight 'o' clock in the evening. His sister Maria Anna Walburga Ignatia alias Nannerl, on the 30th July 1751. They were both born in the so-called "Hagenauer house in the Tragasse", which was built in the 12th century on the grounds of the "St. Petrischer Frauengarten (Saint Peter's garden for women). Mentioned in documents for the first time in the 15th century the building became the property of the court apothecary Chunrad Fröschlmoser in 1585. Above the door there is a reminder of the former owner: the insignia of Aesculapius and the serpent. In the year 1703 the house was purchased by the Hagenauer family, who were middle-class merchants. At that time the facades on both sides of the house were beautifully decorated in Rococo style, but today the original appearance can only be seen on the University Square side. The street front is plain Classicistic in style. In November of 1747 Lorenz Hagenauer rented out an apartment on the third floor to his friend, the newly wed Leopold Mozart. It included (and still

Mozart's birthplace: for 26 years the family lived on the third floor of this house. The apartment consisted of a kitchen, small chamber, study, bedroom and living room.

includes today) a kitchen, a small room, bedroom, living room and a study. It was to be the address of the composer's family until they moved to the "Tanzmeister" house across the river Salzach in 1773.

In 1856 a comprehensive exhibition was held in Mozart's birthplace covering his life and works. Then in 1880 the International Mozarteum Foundation installed a permanent Mozart-Museum in the building, including a number of instruments, pictures, signatures, documents, memorabilia and mementos. Just before the end of World War I the foundation gained possession of the whole house and in 1931 a historical theatre department was added on the second floor.

Johann Lorenz Hagenauer

Mozart used this clavichord (on show in the house where he was born) when he composed The Magic Flute, Clemenza di Tito and the Requiem.

SALZBURG

Probably the most famous – and probably the most beautiful – portrait of the composer: Joseph Lange's unfinished oil painting from 1789.

In the Salzburg Cathedral Mozart's parents were married, he was baptised and many of his works were performed.

On the third floor at the back of the house there is a wonderful example of what living conditions were like for the middle-class citizen in Salzburg in Mozart's day. In the authentically furnished apartment there are numerous objects of interest, besides table and chairs, mirror and wall clock, side-board, wardrobe and pictures, there is also a hammer-clavier and a chamber pot. In the adjoining, original Mozart apartment the collection concentrates mainly on musical instruments and portraits of the family, among which there is the famous, unfinished oil painting by Joseph Lange, that shows the 33 year-old Mozart playing piano.

2 CATHEDRAL
(Domplatz): The monumental, early Baroque edifice was built according to the plans of Santino Solaris. Here on the 21st of November 1747 Mozart's parents, Anna Maria and Leopold, were married and

Mozart received the holy sacrament of baptism at half past ten mid-morning on January the 28th. Mozart composed most of his sacred music, including Masses, Litanies, Propers, church sonatas etc. for the Cathedral's beautiful, light, richly decorated, stuccoed interior. As court organist, which he was for two years from 1779 on, he played the Cathedral's splendid organ, that, with its 120 registers and 10 000 pipes, is the second largest in Austria (after that of St. Stephan's Cathedral in Vienna). The organ-builders Joseph and Johann Christoph Egedacher were responsible for its construction.

3 RESIDENZ
(Residenz Square I): The Archbishop's extensive residential government palace served Mozart many times during his life in Salzburg as a place for performances. This was where he made his first appearance as a piano- and violin playing child prodigy for Prince Archbishop Schrattenbach. And on the occasion of a visit by Archduke Maximilian Franz, Maria Theresia's youngest son, on the 23rd of April 1775, the opera *Il re pastore* was staged here for the first time. In the Hall of Knights, the place where Mozart often performed as a member of the Salzburg court orchestra, the first performance of his early work, the oratorio *Die Schuldigkeit des Ersten Gebots*, was staged on the 12th of March 1767.

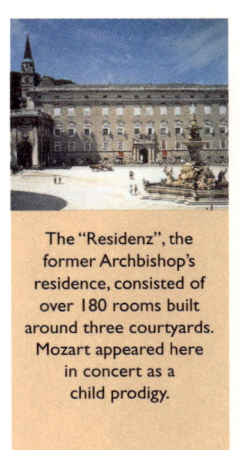

The "Residenz", the former Archbishop's residence, consisted of over 180 rooms built around three courtyards. Mozart appeared here in concert as a child prodigy.

"The Cathedral square and St. Rupert's Cathedral in Salzburg". Painting by Karl Schneeweiß, late 18th century.

From the centre tower of the so-called Residenz-Neugebäude, that was built in 1600 for Archbishop Wolf Dietrich, the glockenspiel rings out melodies at 7, 11 a.m. and 6 p.m. daily. Among the tunes one can hear, there are regular adaptions of Mozart's works. The instrument produces the chimes on its 35 bells the mechanics of which are coordinated by a clock and a cylinder. The piece was purchased by Archbishop Johann Ernst von Thun from a smithy in Antwerp in 1695. It didn't function, however, until about ten years later, when a local clock maker started it working (guided tours: see p. 81).

4 Old University/Main Hall

(Universitätsplatz, Hofstallgasse): The "Alma Mater Paridiana" was founded by Archbishop Paris Count Lodron in 1622. In the festival hall (entrance via Universitätsplatz; through the inner courtyard up the stairs to the first floor) Mozart's earliest stage piece, the school comedy opera *Apollo et Hyacinthus*, was performed for the first time on the 13th of May 1767. As a five-year-old he had already stood in front of an audience, as an extra in the school's Latin drama "Sigismundus Hungariae Rex", on the 1st of September 1761. Prince Archbishop Siegmund Christoph von Schrattenbach (as the man responsible for watching over moral behavoir), had just recently

The University or Kollegien Church. Mozart's *Missa brevis in D minor (K 65)* was first performed here, in 1769.

SALZBURG 60

The ideal site for Mozart's music: Mirabell Palace. The picture shows the staircase with stucco, marble banister and Baroque sculptures by Georg Raphael Donner.

ordered that in theatre performances of this kind, that were especially held for the end of term festivities, sexes should be strictly segregated.

Usually, this splendidly decorated hall is closed, but chances of seeing its interior with its stucco, golden frame-work and rosary pictures arise, when public lectures are held on the University's Open Days, and on the rare occasions when concerts are performed here.

▲ 5 KOLLEGIEN OR UNIVERSITY CHURCH (Universitätsplatz): In Johann Bernhard Fischer von Erlach's magnificent bulbous Baroque building, with its two spires, which borders onto the University complex, the *Missa brevis in D minor (K 65)* (which was written for the festive inauguration of the forty-hour prayer service) was conducted for the first time on the 5th of February 1769.

The view from the Mirabell garden, towards the palace and the old town, is one of the most frequently encountered picture post card panoramas in Salzburg.

■ 6 MIRABELL PALACE:
In the marble hall of the palace, where nowadays Sunday matinées are performed throughout the year, Leopold Mozart and his two children appeared in concert for the Prince Archbishop and his guests. The former country home of Wolf Dietrich von Raitenau, which he had had built in 1606 for his one and only love and mother of his children, the allegedly exceedingly beautiful merchant's daughter, Salome Alt, was restyled in Baroque fashion about a hundred years later by Lukas von Hildebrandt for Markus Sittikus. It

SALZBURG

The Abbey Church of St. Peter's – where the *Dominicus Mass* and *C minor Mass (K 427)* were heard for the first time.

"I am the gate to life. Come and pass through me, those of you that will be saved", thus reads the inscription in the Romanesque arch in the main entrance.

is hard to imagine a more suitable place than this for listening to music.

▲ 7 ABBEY CHURCH OF ST. PETER:
This is the oldest and most venerable of all of Salzburg's churches, its forerunner was constructed under St. Rupert in the 7th century. Around the time of Mozart's birth Abbot Beda Seeauer ordered the High-Romanesque interior to be covered with late-Baroque styled frescoes and stucco. Later Mozart's two most important sacred works were to be heard here for the first time: On the 15th of October 1769 the so-called *Dominicus Mass in C major (K 66)*, which was composed for the first Mass of his childhood friend and newly ordained Father Dominicus (Kajetan Rupert Hagenauer), who became Abbot of St. Peters and was to play an important role in religious life in Salzburg; and on the 26th of October 1783 the unfinished *Mass in c minor (K 427)*, which the Maestro himself conducted, and at which his wife Constanze sang one of the two soprano parts.

In the third chapel in the right-hand nave there is a memorial with a cross, a harp, an urn and a tablet with the brief inscription: "Michaeli Haydn, Nato Die 14. Sept. 1737. Vita Functo Die 10. Aug. 1806". Joseph Haydn's younger brother was interred in the neighbouring St. Peter's cemetery. He was the orchestra leader who took over from Leopold Mozart as a 26 year-old in 1763, and was later given the office of organist and concert master of the Benedictines in the Abbey of St. Peter. In the same chapel there is another memorial plaque in remembrance of Nannerl Mozart. It reads:

"Monument of Marianne Baroness von Berchtold zu Sonnenburg. Daughter of the Princely Salzburg court orchestra leader, Leopold Mozart, Sister of the famous musician and Imperial and Royal court orchestra leader Wolfgang Amadeus Mozart and Wife of the Princely Counciller and Court Assessor in St. Gilgen, Joh. Bapt. Baron von Berchtold zu Sonnenburg, born in Salzburg 30. July 1751, died 29. Oct. 1829.

Placed here as proof of innermost thanks and love by their son Leopold Baron v. Berchtold zu Sonnenberg 'IMP. AND ROYAL MOUNTAIN CLERK IN TYROL'."

During the festival weeks the above mentioned *Mass in c minor* is played, and on the eve of the anniversary of his death, in other words on the 4th of December, the Maestro's *Requiem* can be heard here in this church.

St. Peter's Church and Abbey. When Mozart and his wife visited Salzburg, in 1783, the *C minor Mass* was performed here. Engraving by Klauber, 1780.

The newly constructed "Tanzmeisterhaus" on the Makartplatz, was Mozart's home from 1773 on.

8 MOZART APARTMENT

(Makartplatz 8): When the Mozart family returned from their last Italian and third Vienna trip, their home had definitely become too small for them and they moved to the right bank of the river Salzach. Their new address: the so-called "Tanzmeisterhaus" (Dance Master's House) on the Hannibalplatz (today Makartplatz). The building with the long front, partly one, partly two stories high, received its name from the fact, that since the beginning of the century, the owner, a certain Lorenz Speckner, gave dancing lessons to the aristrocracy. Many of the affluent aristocratic students and their tutors from Salzburg's Benedictine University took lodgings in these premises. The Mozart family lived in a spacious eight-roomed apartment. In the building's large "Tanzmeistersaal" (dance hall), where a few years earlier Michael Haydn had his wedding reception, the Mozarts invited their friends round for music and "Bölzlschiessen" (crossbow shooting at targets with funny pictures), a much favoured pastime in those days. Mozart's father Leopold, who passed away in this domicile in 1787, frequently used the hall for exhibiting the pianos he had received for sale on commission, from the people who built them. Mozart, who lived at this address till August 1780 then came back again for a short stay from August till October 1783, composed over 150 pieces here. Amongst these works were the opera *Il re pastore,* parts of *La finta giardiniera* and

Idomeneo. In 1856, for the hundredth birthday of the composer, a plaque with the words "Mozart's Wohnhaus" (Mozart's Home), was put on the front facade of the house. The Mozart foundation rented three rooms of the former apartment for an exhibition in 1938. And before the outbreak of World War II the house was added to the list of buildings considered worthy of protection by the preservation council. Nevertheless, on the 16th of October 1944, during the first allied forces airraid, the house was almost completely destroyed (only the dance hall survived) by the detonation of a 500 kg bomb. In 1951 a nondescript multi-story office building was erected where the rubble had been.

The Mozarteum Foundation purchased the "House on Makartplatz" in 1989 and started a collection for its authentic reconstruction. On the 26th of January 1996, – after the demolition of the interemistic building and after only two years of construction work supported financially by a Japanese insurance company – the exemplary renovated Tanzmeisterhaus was inaugurated. There are five rooms containing manuscripts and pictures of Mozart and his contemporaries-dedicated in this order to – (room 1), Leopold Mozart's library (2), Nannerl, the sister (3), furniture and requisites from Mozart's surroundings (4), his travels and the new Mozart editions (5). In addition the house offers an informative film about Mozart's life, the Mozart film and music museum, and also, on the ground-floor, a well assorted "Classic Disc Shop".

9 Antretter House

(Mozartplatz 4): The relationship between the family of the Privy Counciller and Country-Chancellor, Johann Ernst Edler von Antretter, and the Mozart family was a friendly one. Leopold reports that Nannerl went "every Thursday to the house of Andretter". Wolfgang most probably also went to play in the Baroque building – once the town palace of the von Rehlingen family – diagonally across from the Café Glockenspiel. The name of the inhabitants went down in music history because of the *Antretter Serenade* (K 185), which Mozart probably composed when Judas Thaddäus Antretter successfully completed his academic

The Glockenspiel in the tower of the Residenz building.

The inner-courtyard of the Antretter house, on Mozartplatz, where young Wolfgang played games and music.

studies. Today only the front one of the two beautiful inner-courtyards can be seen from the inside, the other, rear one, with the house chapel, is private property and can only be seen through the gate at the entrance.

● ▲ 10 ROBINIGHOF
(Robinigstraße 1, near Schallmooser Hauptstraße): The Mozart family were also well acquainted with the iron merchant Georg Josef Robinig von Rottenfeld and his family who came from Villach. Little Wolfgang played with the Robinig children, Maria Aloisia Viktoria and Georg Sigismund both in their town house in today's Sigmund-Haffner-Gasse 14, as well as in their home, the well preserved Robinighof with its splendid Rococo facade, in the suburb of Gnigl. Later on they would make music together. Mozart probably wrote the *divertimento for string quartet and two horns (K 334)* and the *march (K 445)* in 1779 for the regular "eleven 'o' clock concerts" that were held in the Robinighof.

□ 11 ALTES BORROMÄUM
(Mirabellplatz 1): This building, known as the "Lodronischer Primogeniturpalast" dates back to the mid-17th century. It was named after its owner Arch-

bishop Paris Lodron. Mozart did play here now and again, and for Maria Antonia, the wife of the resident hereditary Marshall Ernst Maria Johann Nepomuk Count Lodron, he wrote the two *Nachtmusiken (K 247 and 287)* between 1776 and 1778. It was also for the Countess and her two daughters that Mozart composed the *concerto for three pianos (K 242)*. It is in this palace and the relatively plain, rear wing extension from 1979, the "Mozarteum University of Music and the Performing Arts" is housed. It was built on the site of the former princes pleasure garden and is frequented by music students from all over the world who come here to study. In the entrance hall there is a memorial plaque in honour of the founding members, among others, Carl Orff, Ernst Krenek, Paul Hindemith and Wilhelm Backhaus.

12 HAFFNER HOUSE
(Sigmund-Haffner-Gasse 6): In this Baroque building, recognisable by the medallion of the Virgin Mary above the marble doorway, lived the Haffner family. They belonged to the the Mozart family's closest circle of friends. The head family member was Siegmund Haffner senior, a wholesaler and inofficial banker who supplied Prince Archbishop Schrattenbach with interest-free monies. He later became mayor.

Quite close to the Mozart home in the Tanzmeister house where the family lived from 1773 on: Dreifaltigkeitsgasse (= Trinity Street). Painting by Michael Sattler.

Wolfgang and his children, Sigismund junior and Elisabeth, were very close friends. In the summer of 1776, Mozart composed the *serenade in D major (K250)* for the stag-night of Elisabeth's bridegroom, Franz Xaver Späth. In the year 1782, for the occasion of Siegmund's ennoblement, he composed a second Haffner-Serenade. It was not very much later when he decided to rearrange this piece of music. The main alterations and adjustments to the composition were made (among others) by omitting the march and a menuet. The result of these changes was the *symphony in D major* with four movements *(K 385)*.

The title-page of the *symphony in D major (K 385)*. Composed for the ennoblement of Sigmund Haffner in 1782.

Mozartplatz with the Café Glockenspiel and the bronze monument of the Maestro, by Ludwig Schwanthaler, cast in 1842.

13 KAFFEEHAUS STAIGER
(today: CAFÉ TOMASELLI, Alter Markt 9): Already in the 18th century there was a coffee-house here, which was regularly frequented by Mozart. Today this venue serves the Salzburg society as a meeting place, especially during the festival weeks. Unlike today, however, in Mozart's time, billiards were played and theatre performances were held in the so-called "Staigerischen Caffetterie".

Mozart's rather critical comments about the quality of what was served – he called the caterer a "patron of burning coffee soup, of rotten lemonade, of almond milk without almonds and of strawberry ice-cream full of ice lumps" – he would no doubt not repeat today.

14 ST. SEBASTIAN'S CEMETERY
(Linzergasse): Archbishop Wolf Dietrich von Raitenau closed the old Cathedral Cemetery when the new Cathedral was being built, and had the already existing Sebastian's cemetery redone and enlarged. In the east-part of the square "Campo Santo" enclosure, near the Chapel of St. Gabriel (Raitenau's early Baroque mausoleum), surrounded by 84 arcades, many members of the Mozart family found their last resting place: in 1755 Wolfgang Amadeus Mozart's maternal

Sebastian's cemetery. In the background: the Gabriel Chapel, Wolf Dietrich von Raitenau's mausoleum, designed by Elia Castello.

Grandmother, Eva Rosina Pertl; 1798 Genoveva Weber, Constanze's aunt and the mother of Carl Maria von Weber; 1805 Nannerl's first daughter Johanna Maria Anna Elisabeth von Berchtold zu Sonnenberg; 1826 Georg Nikolaus Nissen Constanze's second husband; and probably of more importance to the visitor, 1842 Constanze, Mozart's widow, and already in 1787 Mozart's father Leopold.

When Leopold died, Abbot Dominicus Hagenauer made a note in his diary: "Whit-Monday, the 28th early, the local vice orchestra leader Leopold Mozart died, with his two children he brought special honour to Salzburg about 20 years ago ... The deceased was a man of much wit and wisdom, He would have served the State well in fields other than music. He ... was unlucky in that he always encountered difficulties here, and was not as esteemed as he was in other large cities in Europe."

15 ZAUBERFLÖTENHÄUSCHEN

(Schwarzstraße 26/28; in the garden of the International Mozarteum Foundation): According to legend Mozart composed part of the *Magic Flute* in this small, wooden pleasure-house in summer of 1791. Rumour has it that Emanuel Schikaneder, the librettist and principal, who saw time running out – the piece was to have its first performance on the 30th September 1791 – locked Mozart inside the edifice to ensure completion of the work. Rumour also has it that Mozart met here with singers to rehearse the various individual roles. Originally located in the garden of the Viennese "Freihaus Theater" otherwise known as "Theater auf der Wieden", the "House of the Magic Flute" was given to the International Mozarteum Foundation by Prince Starhemberg who had sold the "Freihaus" (an extensive tenement building in the Vienna suburb of Wieden) in 1873. At first it stood in the gnomes garden just across from Mirabell Palace, then from 1877 to 1950 it was situated on the Kapuzinerberg, until, after repeated renovations, it found its final location in the Bastion garden of the Mozarteum.

16 St. Peter's Cemetery

In this oldest existing God's acre in the German speaking world, where the steps carved into the mountain lead up to the so-called Catacombs, the bodies of Nannerl Mozart (1751–1829) and Michael Haydn (1737–1806) were laid to rest in the common

Here, in St. Peter's cemetery, the bodies of Santino Solari, Clemens Holzmeister, Richard Mayr, Michael Haydn and Mozart's sister, Nannerl, rest in peace.

vaults. At the foot of a crucifix and a dozen interesting pictures showing the "Dance of Death", there are two memorial plates that mark their graves (see also: St. Peter's Abbey Church). In the side arcades of the crypt there is the Classisistic marble tomb of Johann Lorenz Hagenauer the merchant, who owned the house in the Getreidegasse which was the birthplace of Mozart, and one of the best friends of the Mozart family (Arcade No.16). Further, the tomb of the Haffner family (No. 39), best known for the *serenade* and *symphony (K 250* and *385)* named after them. And buried in the midst of all the graves, is Bernhard Paumgartner (1887–1971), conductor, composer, musicologist, former Mozarteum director and president of the Salzburg Festival.

17 BARISANI HOUSE = NANNERL'S HOME (Sigmund-Haffner-Gasse 12) After the death of her husband in 1801, Mozart's sister Nannerl now widowed Baroness von Berchtold zu Sonnenburg, moved from St. Gilgen to an apartment on the third floor in the house of the Prince's Physician Dr. Silvester Barisani. Here she received many visitors who had been friends of Mozart's, and was to earn a living from giving piano lessons, until she lost her eyesight. Maria Anna "Nannerl" died on the 29th of October 1829. There is a memorial plaque on the facade of the building facing the Universitätsplatz which commemorates this fact. A coincidence was the birth of Mozart's biographer and musicologist Erich Schenk in the same house two generations later in 1902 (died 1974), a commemorative plaque can be found on the front of the building.

A street-musician in front of the Mozart monument:
Art and commerce cooperate closely in Salzburg.

SALZBURG

Constanze Mozart, née Weber (1762–1842) – the Maestro's "beloved wife", who was seldom highly regarded by biographers. Painting by Hans Hansen, 1802.

🏠 18 NONNBERGGASSE 12
(Constanze's Apartment): In 1821 Constanze Nissen, Mozart's widow, and her second husband, the Danish diplomat and Mozart biographer Georg Nikolaus Nissen, moved from Copenhagen to Salzburg and took up quarters here in the so-called Öbstlerhaus south of the Old Town at the foot of the Nonnberg.

🏠 19 ALTER MARKT 11
(Contanze's Apartment): For a short period, 1833, Constanze lived in this beautiful house next to the Café Tomaselli, opposite the Florian fountain surrounded by the pretty wrought iron railings. (Memorial plaque in the entrance to the house).

SALZBURG

The Mozart monument, on the square of the same name, was designed by Ludwig von Schwantaler and cast in bronze by Johann Stiglmaier.

20 Mozartplatz 8

(Constanze's Apartment): Constanze Mozart moved to the house in the north-east corner of the former Canonical court of St. Michael (original name of this square), after the death of her second husband Georg Nikolaus Nissen. A memorial plaque on the facade of the building states: "In this house Mozart's widow Constanze Nissen, neé Weber, died on the 6th March 1842 and on the 26th October 1846 her sister Sophie Haibl, Mozart's devoted nurse during his fatal illness."

21 Mozart Monument

(Mozartplatz): In 1835 Sigmund von Koflern from Salzburg and Juluis Schilling a writer from Posen in Prussia, encouraged the erection of a monument for the great son of the City on the Salzach. But years were to pass till the sculptor from Munich, Ludwig von Schwanthaler, (the author of the "Bavaria" that thrones the bank of the Isar river) designed and finished the Classisistic figure. The Bronze statue was cast in the royal foundry in Munich by Johann Stiglmaier on the 22nd of May, one year after the "Dom-Musik-Verein" and the "Mozarteum" were established. Four months later on the 4th of September 1842 in the presence of the two sons – Constanze had died a few months earlier – the unyeiling ceremony was held. Franz Xaver Wolfgang, also known as Wolfgang Amadeus Mozart (son), conducted a festival cantata that he had composed in honour of his father. A contemporary chronicler found the following words to describe the monument (the state of the statue has hardly changed): "W. A. Mozart wearing the typical dress of his day with the, in those times, customary long-coat. He glances upwards, one foot resting on a rock (his homeland), the right hand holds the stylus, the left a music score. On the front a relief showing an angel with an organ (symbol of sacred music), to the right the side dedicated to his theatre compositions two female figures, in medieval strength, singing, one with her hand on her heart, to her right a figure, in antique dress with a mask and a lyre; left a group of girls and boys, singing and making music (chamber music and

SALZBURG

concerts); at the rear a lyre, surrounded by stars, signifying the apotheosis even more."

22 Mozarteum

(Schwarzstraße 26 and 28): The decision to create a home specially for the "Dom-Musik-Verein und Mozarteum", which became known as the "International Foundation Mozarteum" in 1880, was made on the occasion of the composer's one hundredth birthday. But after a number of unsuccessful attempts, it wasn't until 1907 that a suitable property was purchased. Two years later a competition was held inviting ideas for the construction of a Mozart house at Schwarzstraße 24, once the property of the former minister for home affairs Josef von Lasser. More than sixty architects sent in their plans. The first prize went to the Munich architect Richard Berndl. His plans in the style of Munich's late-Historism, a "Classicistic Art Noveau" design, were realized in the years 1910–14.

In the west wing, which reaches as far as the Schwarzstraße (house No. 28), the large concert hall with a seating capacity of 800, the foyers, rehearsal rooms and artist's dressing rooms are to be found. The bronze statue in the entrance hall was made by Edmund von Hellmer and shows "Mozart as Apollon Musagète". The adjacent school wing stands back somewhat

The "Grand Hall" in the Mozarteum (Schwarzstraße 28). Seating capacity for 800 people, and often the site used for Mozart-Matinées and Salzburg Festival performances.

(No. 26) – easily recognizable by the four young allegorical male figures above the attica – and houses the administrative rooms, the library and the quarters of the foundation's president, which is also the nucleus of Mozart research world-wide. Further, for an audience of around 200, the so-called Vienna Hall and, on the ground floor, the classrooms of the "University for Music and Performing Arts Mozarteum". The architectural pearl of the house is the library on the first floor decorated entirely in Art Nouveau style. This special "Bibliotheca Mozartiana" contains roughly 30 000 titles, including numerous autographed music scores and letters by the Mozart family, first, early and contemporary editions of works by Wolfgang Amadeus and other 18th and 19th century composers.

A Cityscape like a Mozart symphony. In the foreground, the domes and spires of the Kollegien Church by Fischer von Erlach; in the background, the Cathedral.

☐ 23 LANDESTHEATER WITH
MARIONETTENTHEATER (PUPPET THEATRE)
(Schwarzstraße 22 and 24): This theatre, which is to be found immediately after the Mozarteum, was designed by the two architects Ferdinand Fellner and Hermann Helmer and built in the years 1892/93. Originally it was known as the "Stadttheater", and was used for opera performances from the very beginning. Since the end of World War I there was intensive cooperation between the theatre management and the Mozarteum's opera school under director Bernhard Paumgartner, to produce not only, but especially Mozart's stage works. From 1922 for three years, whilst the festival hall was being adapted, the festival's opera performances were held here. Although the house is endowed with a relatively small allocation of state funds (as a provincial theatre) it has nevertheless succeeded in keeping its reputation as a caring protector of the art of opera. There is special reference made to the genius loci in the stage curtain that was designed by A. D. Goltz: it shows the apotheosis of Mozart in the midst of his most famous opera characters.

Located in one of the side wings of the Landestheater is the home of the world famous puppet theatre. The initiative came from the academic sculptor Anton Aicher, who inaugurated the institution in 1913 with a performance of *Bastien and Bastienne* in the the old Borromäum courtyard. The third generation of the Aicher family manages the institution today with a repertoire which besides works from Rossini, Offenbach, Tchaikowsky and Strauß, concentrates especially on the great Mozart operas such as *The Abduction from the Seraglio, Così fan tutte, Marriage of Figaro, Don Giovanni* and *The Magic Flute*.

☕ 24 CAFÉ-KONDITOREI FÜRST
(Brodgasse 13): In 1890 in the confectioner's shop located in the basement of this house the conditor Paul Fürst, after much experimenting, created the first "Mozart Bonbon". He started out by moulding green, pistachio-nut marzipan into a small ball which he covered with a layer of fine nougat, put the whole on the end of a thin stick, which after being dipped in

dark chocolate liquid, was left overnight to drain and dry. Finally, after removing the stick, the hole was closed with some more chocolate and the sweet creation, later to become known as the "Mozart Ball", was wrapped in shiny foil. In 1905 Fürst was to receive a gold medal for his invention at an international exhibition in Paris. The foundation stone for a great culinary career was laid. Today Norbert Fürst, great grandson and proprietor of the premises, continues to produce the delicacy in the traditional way according to the old recipe. But due to the fact that the culinary stroke of genius was never patented by its creator, besides the "original", about a half a dozen imitators roll the, more or less real, Mozart ball onto the world market.

25 Papageno Fountain

(Papagenoplatz): The fountain with the hagard figure of the protagonist from the *Magic Flute*, was made by the Salzburg sculptor Hilde Heger in the year 1960.

26 Mozartsteg

The foot bridge that crosses the Salzach river, level with the "Residenz-Neugebäude", offers a beautiful panorama view, from the foothills of the Gaisberg to the Kapuzinerberg and Mönchsberg mountains, capturing the city's magnificent incomparable landscape in one glance. This is the appropriate place to conjure up the words by Hugo von Hofmannsthal, who wrote the following about this city: "The heart of the heart of Europe, in the centre between North and South, between mountain and plain, between heroic and idyllic. As an edifice between the urban and the rural, ancient and contemporary, between Princely Baroque and charming everlasting ruralism. Mozart is the exact expression of all this. Central Europe has no finer place, and here Mozart had to be born."

MOZART'S SALZBURG - FACTS

Code for Salzburg: 0662
(international: +43-662-)

MUSEUMS, GRAVES AND MEMORIALS:

MOZART'S BIRTHPLACE:
Getreidegasse 9, phone 84 43 13, fax 94 06 93 (daily 9 a.m–6 p.m.; mid-June to early September 9 a.m.–7 p.m)

MOZART APARTMENT
(Tanzmeisterhouse): Makartplatz 8, phone 88 94-940-40 (daily 10 a.m.–6 p.m.; end of June to the end of August 9 a.m.–6 p.m.).
Mozart music and film museum (in the Tanzmeisterhaus): Mon, Tue, Fri 9 a.m.–1 p.m., Wed, Thu 1 p.m.–5 p.m.

MAGIC FLUTE HOUSE
(in the Bastion Garden of the Mozarteum):
Guided tours for groups on request under the phone 87 42 27-40.
The house can be seen from the outside from the southern side of the Mirabell Gardens

ST. PETER'S CEMETERY
(Entrance either south-west corner of the Kapitelplatz or through the Kolleghof, or the outer abbey courtyard): January–March and October–December from early morning to 6 p.m.; April, May and September till 7 p.m.; June–August till 8 p.m.)

SEBASTIEN'S CEMETARY
(Entrance via Linzergasse): April–October 7 a.m.–7 p.m., November–March 7 a.m.–7 p.m.

EVENTS (TICKET SALE/ BOOKINGS)

DOM MUSIC
(Cathedral concerts, organ matinees):
Ticket agents, evening box office

SALZBURG FESTIVAL:
Hofstallgasse 1., P.O box 40, phone 80 45-0, 84 45 01, fax 84 66 82, E-Mail: info@salzb-fest.co.at (Mon–Fri 8 a.m.–12:30 p.m, 1–4:30 p.m.; during the festival: 10 a.m.–12 noon, 3–5 p.m.
Direct sale at the box office of the Festival Hall (during the festival): Mon–Fri 9:30 a.m.–3 p.m. sometimes till 5 p.m.

FORTRESS CONCERTS:
Direktion der Salzburger Festungskonzerte, Anton-Adlgasser-Weg 22, phone 82 58 58, fax 82 58 59 (daily 9 a.m.–9 p.m.), ticket agencies

FRANCISCAN CHURCH:
Mass – entrance free. Organ recitals: see int. organ concerts.
International organ week: in St. Blasius, ticket agencies, box office from 7 p.m.

INTERNATIONAL SALZBURG ORGAN CONCERTS:
ticket agencies, box office.
International Summer Academy "Mozarteum": Mirabellplatz 1., phone 88 908-810 (July/August 10 a.m.–12 noon, 1–4 p.m.), ticket agencies

KULTURTAGE:
Kulturvereinigung, Waagplatz 1a (Mon–Fri 8 a.m.–6 p.m.), phone 84 53 46, fax 84 26 65, ticket agencies

LANDESTHEATER:
Schwarzstraße 22, phone 87 15 12-0, fax 87 15 12-13 (Tue-Fri 10 a.m.–1 p.m., 5:30–7 p.m., Sat 10 a.m.–1 p.m., 5 p.m.–6:30 p.m.)

MARIONETTEN / PUPPET THEATRE:
Schwarzstraße 24 (Mon-Sat 9 a.m.–1 p.m. and 2 hours before performance begins), phone 87 24 06-0, fax 88 21 41, ticket agencies

MOZART DINNER CONCERT & MOZART-MATINEÉ IN SCHLOSS MIRABELL:
Konzertdirektion Steinschaden & Hiller, Anif 348, 5081 Anif, phone 06246/76 11 74, ticket agencies

MOZART CHURCH CONCERTS SALZBURG:
Society of sacred music Salzburg, J.-v.-Eichndorff-Straße 20 (daily 8 a.m.–8 p.m.), phone 82 37 88, fax 82 38 16, ticket agencies, box office: 0663/86 34 15

MOZARTEUM (MOZART WEEK):
Theatergasse (Mon–Thu 9 a.m.–2 p.m., Fri 9 a.m.–4 p.m.), phone 87 31 54, fax 87 29 96; evening box office: phone 88 94026, ticket agencies. Mozart Serenades (Schloß Hellbrunn and Mozarteum): Konzertdirektion Nerat, Lieferinger Hauptstraße 136 (daily 9 a.m.–9 p.m.), phone 43 68 70, 0664/20 34 700, fax 43 69 70, ticket agencies, evening box office

OPERA IN THE HECKENTHEATER:
see Mozart Dinner Concert.

RESIDENZ-MOZART-MATINEES:
Salzburg Special, Pegiusgasse 5a
(Mon–Fri 3–7 p.m.), phone 82 47 05,
fax 82 72 03, ticket agencies

SALZBURG CONCERTS:
phone 06212/62 07-4 (bookings by
phone only)

SALZBURG ADVENT
(in the University/Kollegien church):
ticket agencies

SALZBURG KAMMERPHILHARMONIE:
Concert office – Henry-Dunant-
Straße 16/1, phone 62 78 96,
fax 62 78 96-4, ticket agencies

SALZBURG SCHLOSSKONZERTE:
Konzertdirektion, Griesgasse 6/1
(Mon–Fri 9 a.m.–5 p.m.), phone
84 85 86, fax 84 47 47, ticket
agencies

TURMBLASEN IN ADVENT:
Residenzplatz. Entrance free of charge

**BOOKS, NOTES,
DOCUMENTS ETC.:**

INTERNATIONAL MOZARTEUM
FOUNDATION LIBRARY:
Schwarzstraße 26 (Mon–Fri 9 a.m.–
12 noon and 2–5 p.m.),
phone 88 940-13

MOREOVER:

SALZBURG GLOCKENSPIEL
(in the Residenz-Neugebäude):
Guided tours (possibly from March
1997 on) April–October daily at
10:45 a.m. and 5:45 p.m.
(1. November–end of March work-
days only). No tours when inclement
weather. Meeting point in the house
entrance on Mozartplatz 1

MARBLE HALL IN SCHLOSS MIRABELL:
If no weddings are held, entrance free
Mon, Wed and Thu 8:30 a.m.–
4 p.m., Tue and Fri 1-4 p.m.

**WELL ASSORTED
BOOK SHOPS:**

HÖLLRIGL,
Sigmund-Haffner-Gase 10,
phone 84 11 46

MAYRISCHE MISIKALIENHANDLUNG
(also scores): Theatergasse,
phone 87 35 96

DOM BUCHHANDLUNG,
Kapitelplatz 6, phone 84 21 48

RUPERTUS,
Dreifaltigkeitsgasse 12,
phone 87 87 33-0

MORA,
Residenzplatz 2, phone 84 36 20

STIERLE,
Kaigasse 1/ Mozartplatz
phone 84 01 14

CLASSICAL MUSIC CDS:

Katholnigg,
Sigmund-Haffner-Gasse 16,
phone 84 14 51

Classic Disc
(in Mozart's apartment),
Makartplatz 8, phone 88 45 42-0

Music Mirabell,
Rainerstr. 2, phone 87 5 7 75-0

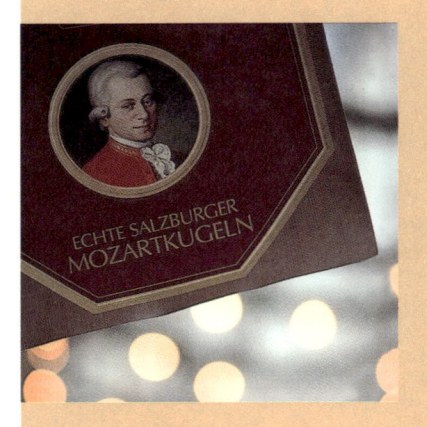

COFFEE HOUSES:

Café Tomaselli:
Alter Markt 9 (daily except Sun. and holidays 7 a.m.–8:30 p.m.),
phone 84 44 88

Café Glockenspiel:
Mozartplatz 2 (daily 9 a.m.–7 p.m.),
phone 84 14 03

Café Bazar:
Schwarzstraße 3 (Mon 10 a.m.–6 p.m., Tue-Sat 7:30 a.m.–11 p.m., Sun closed.), phone 87 42 78

MOZARTKUGELN:

Café and confectioners Fürst
(the original): Brodgasse 13,
phone 84 37 59.
Other variations offered by:
Mirabell, Reber, Hofbauer, Hofer,
Schmidt and Meinl

GENERAL TOURIST INFORMATION:

Salzburg Information:
Direktion, Administration –
Auerspergstraße 7, A-5020 Salzburg,
phone 88 98 7-0, fax 88 98 7-32,
E-mail: tourist@salzburginfo.or.at
(Mon–Thu 8 a.m.–4 p.m.,
Fri 8 a.m.–3 p.m.)

Further Information
at: Information Mozartplatz:
Mozartplatz 5, phone 88 98 7-330;
Main railway station: platform 2a,
phone 88 98 7-340 or 87 17 12;
Salzburg-Mitte: Münchner
Bundesstraße 1, phone 88 98 7-350
or 43 22 28; Salzburg-Süd: Park &
Ride, Alpensiedlung-Süd,
Alpenstraße, phone 88 98 7-360;
Airport: Arrival hall,
phone 85 12 11, 85 20 91 or 85 80-999, fax 85 34 59 (all year round);
Salzburg Nord: Autobahnstation/-motorway stop Kasern,
phone 88 98 7-370 (Easter–31st October)

Salzburg Guide Service:
Pfeifergasse 3/1, phone 84 04 06,
fax 84 54 70

PRAGUE

LOOKING FOR MOZART IN PRAGUE

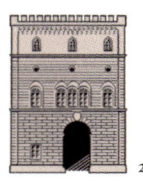

1. Former New Gate
2. Thun Palace or the House of the Iron Gate
3. Bretfeld Palace or House of Summer and Spring
4. Clementinum
5. Estates Theatre
6. Parliament building former Thun-Palais
7. „To the Golden Angel"
8. Church of St. Simon und Judas
9. Nostitz Palace
10. Pachta Palace
11. Schönborn Palace
12. Vrtba Palace
13. Mysliveček Birthplace
14a. Canal Palace
14b. Buquoy Palace
14c. Hummel House
14d. Straka-Nedabylice- Palace
14e. Hartig Palace
14f. St. Vitus Cathedral
15. „To the Three Golden Lions"
16. Platteis House
17. Bertramka (p. 100)
18. „To the Golden Eagle"
19. Strahov Monastery
20. Tein School
21. Saxony House
22. „To the Blue Grape"
23. „To the Three Fiddles"
24. St. Nikolas Church
25. „To the White (Golden) Unicorn"
26. Carolinum
27. Trčka House
28. Lesser Town Cemetery

▲ Première Venues
■ Performance Venues
🏠 Lodgings
◉ Places of important encounters
⚘ Birth
☠ Death
☕ Cafés & Restaurants
▮ Monuments & Memorials

Street names visible on map

- Na Františku
- Kozí
- Dušní
- Pařížská
- 17.listopadu
- Kaprova
- U radnice
- Staroměstské nám.
- Celetná
- Platnéřská
- Železná
- Karlova
- Křižovnická
- Anenská
- Havelská
- Rytířská
- Na Příkopě
- Skořepka
- Národní

Map markers

8, 14a, 7, 20, 1, 27, 26, 5, 4, 22, 13, 10, 16, 15, 17, 24

0 — 500

1 Former New Gate

(New town, today: Senovážné náměstí):
One episode that is still readily told today: It was noon on the 11th of January, 1787, when Mozart, in the company of his wife, his future brother-in-law, Franz Hofer, and the clarinetist Anton Paul Stadler, drove into Prague for the first time. When he stopped for passport control at the New Gate, which stood at the end of the Senovážné náměstí Square in those days, he was asked by the customs officer if he was "the Mr Mozart who had composed the 'Figaro'. When he answered in the affirmative, all those standing around beamed and surprised him with a resounding "You are most heartily welcome!" And a little later, as the travellers rolled along through the Old Town in the carriage of Count Thun, – it was Thun who had invited them to Prague, again and again they heard people singing and whistling the tunes from *Figaro*, especially the theme tune of the aria 'Non più andrai …'". Just a short while before, the English music historian Charles Burney had stated, in the much appraised account of his travels through Europe, that "inhabitants of the Bohemian lands possessed a special, spontaneous musical sense". For the time being, the greatest composer on the Continent had just been given a taste of their enthusiasm and unconditional admiration. He felt this was – and he was right – a good omen. When Mozart said his last goodbye, four years later, he sighed, "My people of Prague really understand me …"

Prague had – according to Mozart – "a society of great lovers and connoisseurs of music", he felt very well there, indeed.

PRAGUE

This copper engraving, by Martin Engelbrecht, shows the former Thun Palace, todays Parliament building on the Lesser Side, (see: 6 Parliament building).

2 THUN PALACE
OR THE HOUSE OF THE IRON GATE

(Lesser Town, Thunovská 14/180*): Mozart's first host and most important patron in Prague, to whom he had dedicated his symphony in *C major, K 425* (composed during his stay in Linz in 1783 and later known as the Linzer symphony), was Count Johann Joseph Thun. According to Mozart's biographer, Franz Xaver Niemetschek, this was the "noble cavalier and music expert who had his own splendid orchestra", that gave the Mozarts "board and lodging and all comforts" in this Palace during the first eight days of their stay. Today the magnificent Renaissance building together with its beautiful park, also known as Leslie-Palace, serves Great Britain as an Embassy.

* These numbers refer to the chronological order of the historic origin of the buildings in the respective districts. These numbers can be seen on the red enamel signs on the facade of each object.

3 BRETFELD PALACE
OR HOUSE OF SUMMER AND SPRING

(Lesser Town, Nerudova 33/243): On the evening of their arrival, the Mozarts went to a ball held in the Palace of Johann Baron von Bretfeld. This man, – a lawyer, from time to time rector of the local university and an avid collector of paintings and books – held frequent dance evenings for the cream of the Prague society in his splendid Baroque Palace in the Ostruhová like many other aristocrats in this city of art. It was on this evening that Mozart made the acquaintance of

Giacomo Casanova

PRAGUE

Beaumarchais' comedy, "Le mariage de Figaro" (in which he ridiculed the state of affairs in the Ancien Régime), was welcomed by the people, but not by the rulers. The engraving by C. N. Malapeau shows a scene from the 1st act, copied from a picture by Jaques de Saint-Quentin, 1785.

Giacomo Casanova, who, since 1785, had lived in the Castle of Waldstein in the north Bohemian town of Duchcov as a librarian. A few days later Mozart wrote a letter to his friend, Gottfried Jacquin, in Vienna, telling him how much he had enjoyed watching "the beautiful elite of Prague society" at the party and how "everybody was dancing and hopping to the music of my Figaro with so much sincere joy, because here there is no other topic of conversation than Figaro, nothing else is played, blown, sung or whistled. Undoubtedly a great honour for me".

4 CLEMENTINUM

(Old Town, Karlova = Křižovnická): On the 13th of January Mozart paid a visit to the Clementinum, the former Jesuit College that had been desecularised by Joseph II in 1773, and which was to become the property of Prague University three years later. Mozart was shown through the house by its director, the Freemason, Raphael Ungar, who took him to see the natural history collection and the library with its enormous collection of 130 000 volumes.

Later a Mozart hall was installed in the building-complex, in the Chapel formerly dedicated to the patron of goldsmiths, Saint Eligius. A few of the composer's manuscripts are kept there, although nowadays the lovely Rococo styled room is more often than not locked.

5 ESTATES THEATRE

(Old Town, Železná II = Ovocný trh): The Royal City "of a hundred spires" on the Moldau river, with a population of about 80 000 in Mozart's day – amongst which many enlightened aristocrats and educated middle-class citizens were to be found, – had three big theatres at that time: the Kotzen Theatre, built in 1737 in the Rytířská/Knights' Street behind the Havel church, where operas were frequently staged; the Thun Theatre in the Lesser Town (see: 6 Parliament building) and the "Count Nostitz National Theatre"

The Estates Theatre (in Czech: Stavovské divadlo) was the venue that saw the legendary performance of *Don Giovanni*. Coloured engraving by Leopold Peukert, c. 1793.

from 1783. The highest ranking feudal lord in the kingdom of Bohemia, Franz Anton Count Nostitz-Rieneck, a passionate music-lover and patron, had had his architect, Anton Haffenecker, plan an adorable box theatre in the heart of the Old Town. The building on Kolin Square (today: Fruit market) was designed in pure Classic style and was opened with a piece fitting for a patron with such enlightened ambitions: Lessing's "Emilia Galotti".

At first under the direction of the impresario Karl Wahr, then a little later under his successor Pasquale Bondini and chief producer and singer Domenico Guardasoni, the house was soon to become the leading theatre in the city. A legendary occasion was the premier performance of the *Marriage of Figaro* in December of 1786, about which Niemetschek reports: "The enthusiasm that was shown by the audience was just incomparable, never before was there anything like it; one could not hear enough of it …"

There was another boost of Mozart-mania on the 19th of January, 1787 when the Maeatro himself performed the symphony in *D major (K 504)* better known as the *Prague symphony,* with the theatre's own orchestra, and then the next day conducted a repeat performance of Figaro. The legendary climax of this Mozart-mania was reached on the 29th of October 1787 when, after frequently being postponed and under, what would be considered today, mean conditions, the first performance of *Don Giovanni* was staged in the Nostitz theatre. The Prague newspaper

The performance of Mozart's *Il dissoluto punito ossia il Don Giovanni* "per la prima volta" on the 9th of October 1787, in the National Theatre of the Counts Nostitz, – later known as the Estates Theatre – was a date of major importance in the history of opera.

PRAGUE

92

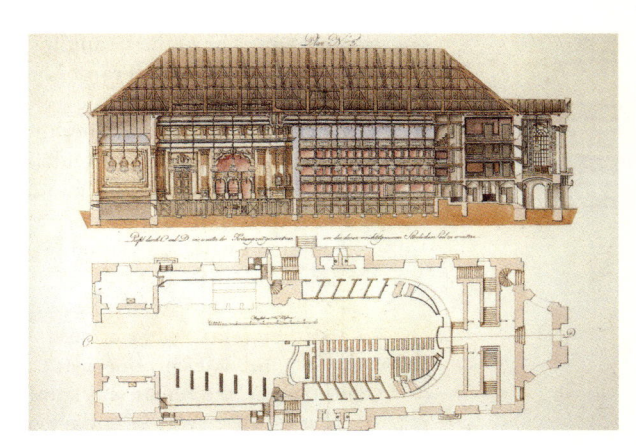

The National – or Estates – Theatre is a jewel of Classisistic architecture. The Copper engraving by Joh. Berka shows the ground plan and profile of the building. Copied from the original by Philip and Franz Heger, 1793.

enthused: "Monday, the 29th, eagerly awaited by all, the opera by Maestro Mozard (sic!) 'Don Giovanni' was performed by the Italian Opera Society. Experts and musicians alike say, that Prague has never experienced anything similar before. Mozard himself conducted, and as he entered the orchestra pit, a threefold cheer was given, which was to be repeated in just the same manner when he left."

On the 6th of September 1791 the house was to stage another of Mozart's works for the first time. It was the opera seria *La clemenza di Tito* commissioned by the Estates, that the already ailing Maestro had composed in just seven weeks for the occasion of the coronation of Emperor Leopold II as King of Bohemia.

At first sight the history of the theatre building, that changed its name frequently, seems rather complicated: When Count Nostitz experienced financial problems it was sold in 1799 to the Bohemian Estates and called "Estates Theatre". Later it became the "Royal District Theatre", and in 1948 it was named after the man who wrote the national anthem of the Czech Republic, Josef Kajetán Tyl and became the "Tyl Theatre". In 1983 the house in which Carl Maria Weber and Gustav Mahler were orchestra leaders, where Clara Schuhmann played piano, Richard Wagner conducted and the first performance of the Czech opera "The Tinker" by Franzisek Skroup was performed, was closed for complete re-

Emperor Leopold II, Mozart composed *La clemenza di Tito* for his coronation festivities in 1790. Engraving by Mechel, 1790.

construction. But just before the closure, Milos Forman had shot some key-scenes in the interior for his film "Amadeus". And since the Jubilee Year of 1991, when the completely renovated building was re-opened with a performance of *Don Giovanni*, the building changed its name once again, almost right back to the beginning, to "Stavovské divadlo", that is – Estates Theatre.

6 PARLIAMENT BUILDING
former THUN PALACE (Lesser Town, Sněmovní 4/176): A few paces from their Palace in Thun Street (see: 2 Thun Palace), in the outgoing 18th century, the Thun family owned another imposing Palace. The building, which was adapted in Neo-Classical style around 1800, became the seat of the Bohemian District Council. From 1918 on the sessions of the newly constituted Senate of the Czech Republic were held here, (there is a commemorative plaque to document this), and for a few years now the Democratic Parliament of the Czech Republic has used this building for holding its meetings. In the days of Mozart's first Prague sojourn, it contained within its walls the "Thun Theatre on the square of the five churches", as well as the Bondini-Society. The impresario, Pasquale Bondini, together with his company, was to keep up the tradition of the Italian opera here, and in the recently completed Nostitz-Theatre. But he broke with tradition by introducing German comedy opera namely the *Abduction from the Seraglio,* and especially the *Marriage of Figaro* to the people of Prague.

7 "TO THE GOLDEN ANGEL"
(Old City, Celetná 29/588, corner Rybná): On the 18th of January 1787, the eighth day of their stay in Prague, the Mozarts moved from the Thun Palace to the tavern called "The New Tavern/Nová Hospoda" in the Zeltnergasse – probably in order to be closer to the Nostitz-Theatre, where Wolfgang Amadeus was rehearsing his *D major symphony K 504,* (the so-called *Prague symphony*) for its first performance. It was here that he is supposed to have composed the *Impromptu (K appendix 207a)* – for the Harpist Joseph Häusler, who could not read music, but knew how to improvise

The Golden Angel, in the picture, is above the entrance to the house of the same name. Mozart stayed here in 1787.

ingeniously by ear. After hearing the melody, Häusler promptly delivered seven variations of it on the strings of the Harp – just like that.

The Classisistic building, which replaced the tavern in 1840, without leaving any reminders of Mozart's stay, served the Prague rebellion in 1848 as garrison headquarters, and later housed the Russian anarchist and revolutionary, Michail Bakunin.

8 CHURCH OF ST. SIMON AND JUDAS (Old City, U milosrdných): In the church belonging to the building complex of the Hospitalers, both Mozart and Joseph Haydn played the organ that still exists and functions today. In the meantime the church has been desecularised and adapted as a concert hall.

9 Nostitz Palace

(Lesser Town, Maltézské náměstí 1/471): The home of the noble family whose name became immortal in music history with the building of the theatre (see: 5 Estates Theatre) of the same name, was also the scene of one of Mozart's visits. Kept at that time in the mighty building dating back to 1660, was the legendary Nostitz private library and the picture gallery. Josef Dobrovský was employed here as a tutor. This was the learned Slav literature teacher and author of the first German-Czech dictionary, whose memorial bust stands opposite the Liechtenstein Palace just a few steps away. Mozart met him in the house of Count Pachta during a soirée in January of 1787. For the time being a wing of the Nostitz Palace is being used by the Dutch as their Embassy. And in another section, in the so-called Empire Salon, regular (Mozart) concerts are performed for the public.

10 Pachta Palace

(Old City, Anenské náměstí/4/208): This was another one of the noble addresses where Mozart paid a musical visit. In this case his hosts were Major General Johann Joseph Philipp Count Pachta von Rájow and his wife Josephine. There is a nice anecdote connected to this house, which Casanova, by the way, also visited: At the beginning of 1787, after the head of the house, having repeatedly reminded Mozart of an order he had given him for some dance music, and after the composer, having had no time to write any, had failed to deliver, had had Mozart locked in a room with paper and writing utensils until the task was successfully completed. The fruits of what was allegedly only one hour of detention, which is supposed to have amused the man no end, were: the six *German Dances K 509*.

In the adjoining "Balustrade Theatre" ("Na zábradlí", No. 5/209) by the way, President Vaclav Havel was forced to work as a stage hand for many years under the communist regime. Later many of his works were first performed here.

11 SCHÖNBORN PALACE
(Lesser Town, Vlašská/Italian Street 15/365):
There is a record which documents that, in this 18th century Baroque Palace, which the aristocratic Schönborn family had bought from the Colloredos, and which today serves the United States of America as an Embassy, Mozart appeared in concert during his first days in Prague in January of 1787.

There was a large community of Italian artists living here, hence the name of the street.

12 VRTBA PALACE
(Lesser Town, Karmelitská 25/373): Here, in the Renaissance Palace of Count Vrtba, who was a close friend of the Duscheks, Mozart was also to demonstrate his stupendous skills as pianist and violinist in front of a small circle of aristocrats in January of 1787.

13 MYSLIVEČEK BIRTHPLACE
(Old Town, Novotného lávka 1/201): Here on the banks of the Moldau, next to the Charles' Bridge, in one of the so-called old city mills that lined the banks of the river in those days, Joseph Mysliveček was born on the 9th of March 1737. As the composer of many operas, oratories, symphonies etc. he had found fame in Italy where he was known and loved as "Il divino Boemo". Mozart had already made his acquaintance in Bologna in 1770, and had then met him again in Milan and Munich. Mysliveček's music had been an inspiration for the juvenile Mozart, and his repeated urging eventually convinced the adult Mozart to travel to Prague. In 1787, six years after the fatherly friend had died, Mozart is supposed to have played the violin here together with

The "Divine Bohemian" Joseph Mysliveček.

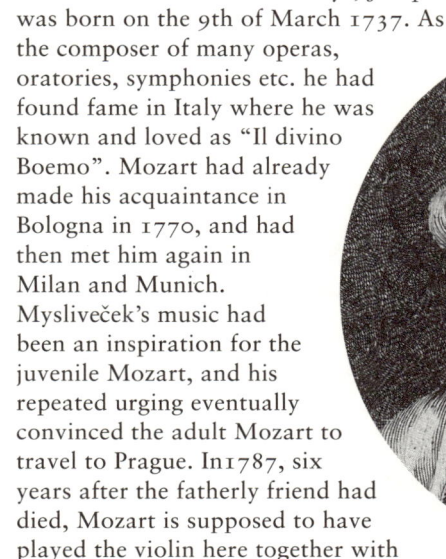

Johann, Joseph's twin-brother. Today in the Neo-Renaissance house, which was built where the mills once stood about a hundred years ago, there is a "Museum for Czech Music". It is closed, and has been for years, the reason is not known. But there is a memorial plaque on the facade for the "divine Bohemian". A few steps further on Friedrich Smetana – cast in bronze and larger than life – waves in greeting across the river up to the Hradschin.

14 FURTHER ADDRESSES
where Mozart most probably appeared in concert: Most of the rich aristocrats in Prague had their own music salons and entertained their guests with a private orchestra, and the likes of a composer such as Mozart will have been passed around from one circle to the next. Soon after his arrival he was most likely demonstrating his genius in the palaces of the aristocracy – and on the organs in most of the important churches. Besides the above mentioned appearances he made in palaces and theatres that have been documented by authentic sources, there were other performances that, most probably, were given in the following places: 14a CANAL PALACE (New Town, Hybernská): Count Canal von Malabaila, an influential Freemason and patron

The view shows the place where Joseph Mysliveček was born in March 1737, at Novotný 1, on the Moldau. He was a composer and a friend of Mozart. (In the background: Charles' Bridge and Hradschin).

The river bank on Lesser Side; in the background the Strahov Monastery and the Hradschin. Etching by Joseph Gregory, copied from Ludwig Kohl, 1793.

organised, like Thun, Pachta and Bretfeld etc. many musical soirées in his long since demolished Palace in the New Town. His botanic garden – beyond the walls of the New Town near the Steed Gate – was, thanks to the concert pavillion in it, an immensely popular meeting place for the music-loving aristocracy; 14b BUQUOY PALACE (Lesser Town, Velkopřevorské náměstí 2/486); 14c HUMMEL HOUSE on the Kampa-, the Devil's Island (Hroznová 7/500); 14d STRAKA-NEDABYLICE-PALACE (Lesser Town, Maltézské náměstí 14/476); 14e HARTIG PALACE (Malostranské náměstí 12/259 = Tržiště 18) and 14f ST. VITUS CATHEDRAL on the Hradschin.

15 "TO THE THREE GOLDEN LIONS" (Old Town, Uhelný trh 1/420): The Mozarts resided here twice in this two-storey house on the corner of Coal Market and Martin/Peel Street in January and October of 1787. The house was the property of the Duschek couple. There is a plaque on the facade above the first floor that says: "U tomto dome bydlil Mozart u roce 1787" (Mozart stayed in this house in the year 1787). Beneath it there is a medallion with the portrait of the famous guest placed there in 1956 to commemorate the bi-centenary of his birth.

Host and much admired singer, Josepha Duschek. Copper engraving by J. F. August Clar, copied from J. F. Haake, 1796.

PRAGUE

The 19th century medallion (painting behind glass), shows Mozart in the home of the Duscheks. Josepha Duschek was an inspiration to her guest.

16 PLATTEIS HOUSE

(Old Town, Uhelný trh 11/416): Here, in the oldest tenement house in the city right across from the "Three Golden Lions", the raffish runaway priest, book-merchant, spy and play-writer Emmanuele Pinkerle-Conegliano alias Lorenzo Da Ponte, stayed for one week from the 8th of October 1787. This bon vivant, who had already finshed the text book for the *Marriage of Figaro,* had come to Prague with the composer as was usual in those days, to finish the libretto for *Don Giovanni,* before the premiere performance, and "to rehearse the roles with the actors", as he was later to remark in his memoirs. There is a cute story one can hear from guides and music historians who have a tendency to tell this kind of anecdote: The composer and the librettist conversed with each other about the progress of their work from one window to the other. In the last century there was a concert hall in the extensive Classisistic building, in which Franz Liszt performed in 1840 and 1846. Today in the building there is a shop with the original name "U Mozarta".

A view of the Villa Bertramka from 1830. Here in the vineyard surrounded, country home of the Duscheks, Mozart was always given a hearty welcome.

17 BERTRAMKA

(Prague 5, Smíchov, Mozartova 2/169): The Bertramka Villa in today's working-class district of Smíchov is, besides the Estates Theatre (see: 5 Estates Theatre), definitely the most important Mozart memorial in Prague. The property, once in an idyllic setting, formed part of the vineyards of the old Carthusian monastery of St. Mary. Around 1700, a citizen from the Lesser Town, Johann Franz Pimskorn, built a country home there. After numerous changes of ownership, the singer, Josepha Duschek, purchased the premises on the 23rd of April 1784. She had met and befriended Mozart and his family in the summer of 1777, whilst appearing in concert with her husband Franz Xaver, an active pianist, piano-teacher and composer, in Salzburg. When Wolfgang Amadeus and Constanze came to Prague at the beginning of October 1787, to prepare the first performance of *Don Giovanni*, they stayed with the Duscheks in their country home. They had been urging them to come to the city on the Moldau for a long time. It was here, in the quiet of the countryside, where he completed – partly in the corner room, partly on the stone table in the adjoining garden – the full score of the new opera. The weeks in Prague before and after the premier performance, he indicated in retrospect, were the happiest of his whole life.

There is an anecdote that can be heard in connection with the Villa Bertramka: On the 3rd of November Josepha Duschek locked Mozart in one of her garden pavillions with pen and paper, to force him to compose

Entrance and villa today. This is the most important Mozart memorial in Prague.

the concert aria he had been promising her for a long time. Mozart was to repay her for the joke with the immortal *Bella mia fiamma (K 528)*, which he threatened to destroy should Josepha not sing the harmoniously daring composition the first time round without making one single mistake. Fortunately the singer's Prima-Vista talent saved the piece from eradication.

When Mozart came back to Prague, in late-August 1791, for the production of the coronation opera *La clemenza di Tito*, he was to stay once again in the Villa Bertramka.

For the 200th birthday of the prominent guest in 1956, a quite remarkable museum was installed in the premises. It documents, with numerous original manuscripts, paintings and objects, Mozarts activities in Prague, the cultural life at that time and the reception his works were given. Lately regular chamber music concerts have been held in the Sala terrena – and in summer in front on the terrace .

18 "To the Golden Eagle"

(Lesser Town, Malostranské náměstí 14–5/ 203–204, corner Zámecká): Where the building with the pharmacy inside stands today, there was, in those days, one of the town houses that the Duscheks owned. Mozart was a frequent visitor, but not once stayed overnight.

The Lesser Side Ring as seen by Mozart. Left: the St. Nikolaus Church, where faithful Prague friends held a memorial church service on the 14th December 1791. Coloured engraving by Joseph Gregory, 1794.

The south face of the Old Town Ring, seen from the Town Hall tower. Already in Mozart's day this was the heart of the city on the right-bank of the River Moldau.

◉ ☐   19 STRAHOV MONASTERY
(Strahovské nádvoří/Strahov Square):
In November 1787, shortly before Mozart returned to Vienna, he and Josepha Duschek visited the Premonstratensian Monastery that was founded in 1140 and was especially renowned for its enormous library. In the Maria Ascension church he was first given the opportunity of hearing the organ being played by the music director of the Monastery, Norbert Ignaz Lehmann. It was after all the biggest instrument of its kind in the city, with 3 087 pipes and 41 registers. Mozart was, as Lehmann's account tells, to "get the urge to pound the organ himself. He sat on the seat and 'pleno choro' for four minutes made magnificent accords whereby every expert could tell that he was more than just a mean organist". Lehmann later put to paper what he could remember from the improvisation Mozart had pounded out, a fragment of 57 beats, which was to become the *organ phantasy K 528a*.

The Tein Church and Tein School: students from the former Jesuit College, that was once located here, sang in the performance of *Don Giovanni* – very successfully.

◉   20 TEIN SCHOOL
(Old Town, Staroměstské náměstí 14/604):
The house in front of the church of the same name with its beautiful Renaissance gable and Baroque Virgin Mary picture, housed a Jesuit college in the 18th century. Many of the students from the faculty for philosophy that lived here, sang in the first performance

of the *Don Giovanni* opera. One of them is remembered by name, František Hek was to receive twenty farthings from Mozart, who praised him highly for his great effort.

21 SAXONY HOUSE

(Lesser Town, Mostecká 3/55): When rehearsals were over in the Nostitz Theatre and Mozart walked back over the Charles' Bridge towards the Villa Bertramka, he would either go down the wooden steps in front of the Lesser Town Bridge Tower to the main square on the Kampa Island, stop at one of the taverns there, and then continue on his way along the arm of the Moldau, past the many mills – or he would go straight ahead to the Saxony House on Bridge Street.

In the building that was originally Gothic, then adapted in Renaissance style, (Emperor Charles IV had at one time presented this house to Rudolph I the Duke of Saxony) a certain Mr. Stamitz ran a coffee house that was still favoured by artists in the 19th century.

22 "TO THE BLUE GRAPE"

(Old City, Železná 22, corner Havelská): There was once, where the brick-built "Gründerzeit" house stands today, a wine tavern called The Blue Grape. This was frequented by actors and singers from the near-by Nostitz Theatre and Mozart as well. One generation later, in the years between 1813–16, another frequent guest was the young orchestra leader Carl Maria von Weber.

23 "TO THE THREE FIDDLES"

(Lesser Town, Nerudova 12/210): In this house, that since 1667 had belonged to the widow of a well-known lute-maker and in whose courtyard a certain Thomas Edlinger kept a famous violin workshop, Mozart quenched his thirst many a time. The name of the tavern has remained unchanged, in Czech "U tří housliček", and is elucidated by the medallion on the facade, with the three violins in a frame.

The Nikolaus Church – where the people of Prague could often see Mozart's works performed. And after his death, in memory, the *Requiem*.

◻ 24 St. Nicolas Church
(Lesser Town, Malostranské náměstí): On the 14th of December 1791, nine days after Mozart's death, the funeral service was held in this magnificent Baroque edifice, built by Kilian Ignaz Dientzenhofer some sixty years earlier. The requiem was by Anton Rössler, the musical director was Josef Strohbach, frequently the orchestra leader at Mozart's earlier performances, and the singer was Josepha Duschek

But many times when Mozart was still alive his works could be heard here, as well as in other large churches in the city. One *Mass,* probably the Mass in *C minor K 427,* was celebrated (organised by his admirers) on the 6th of December 1787, just three weeks after Mozart had left Prague for Vienna. And just one day before Mozart was at last given the post of Imperial and Royal Court Composer by the Emperor Joseph II.

25 "TO THE WHITE (GOLDEN) UNICORN"

(Lesser Town, Lázeňská/Badgasse 11/285 = Maltézské náměstí 15/603): This palatial-like building, the result of joining two medieval houses together, which was considered to be one of the three best hotels in Prague, was where Mozart stayed on the 10th of April 1789, for one night, with his fellow Freemason, Prince Karl Lichnowsky, on their way to Berlin.

Seven years later Prince Lichnowsky was to stay here again. This time for a longer period and this time in the company of Ludwig van Beethoven. As a reminder there is a bust of the composer next to the main entrance of the building.

26 CAROLINUM

(Old City, Ovocný trh 3/541 = Železná 9): From the year 1383 on until today this oldest and most

Little seems to have changed since the 18th century in the Old Town district of Prague. An enchanting medley of styles, from Gothic and Renaissance to Baroque and Gründerzeit.

The incomparable city of steeples and spires, domes and gabled roofs — where Mozart lived, made music, froliced and feasted.

venerable university building in Europe has served its original purpose. It was here that the faculty of law's music society held a concert in Mozart's memory on the 7th of February 1794. Josepha Duschek was one of the performers.

27 TRČKA HOUSE
(Old Town, Staroměstské náměstí 15/603 = Celetná 1): Built originally in Romanesque style, then adapted in the early Classisistic period during the outgoing 18th century, this building was known in some sources as the "House of the White Unicorn". Here the apothecary Antonín Vojtěch Hampacher's daughter, Josepha Duschek, was born on the 6th of March 1754.

28 LESSER TOWN CEMETERY
= Malostranský hřbitov (Smíchov, Plzeňská třida): This God's acre was opened in a former vineyard, in 1680 during a plague epidemic. It was to be used one hundred years later, according to the reforms of the Josephine era, especially by the communities of the Lesser Town and the Hradschin. This is where the Duschek couple was buried. The modest grave can be found at the left-hand, rear-side, (seen from the entrance), directly on the southern border fence. The inscription on the oval gravestone reads: "Friends and hosts of Wolfgang Amadeus

Mozart in Prague. Owners of Bertramka. František Duschek, Composer, born 8. December 1731, died 12. February 1799.; Josepha Duschkova, born Hampacherova, Singer, born 6. March 1754 in Prague, died 8. January 1824 in Prague". The graveyard, on today's main road leading westwards out of Prague, seems rather similar to the St. Marx Cemetery (where Mozart found his last resting place) in Vienna, with its old trees, the all together somewhat neglected Biedermeier grave-stones and its rather melancholy atmosphere.

A historical view of the Hradschin in Prague. In the centre of the picture: the St. Vitus Cathedral – where Mozart most probably played the organ.

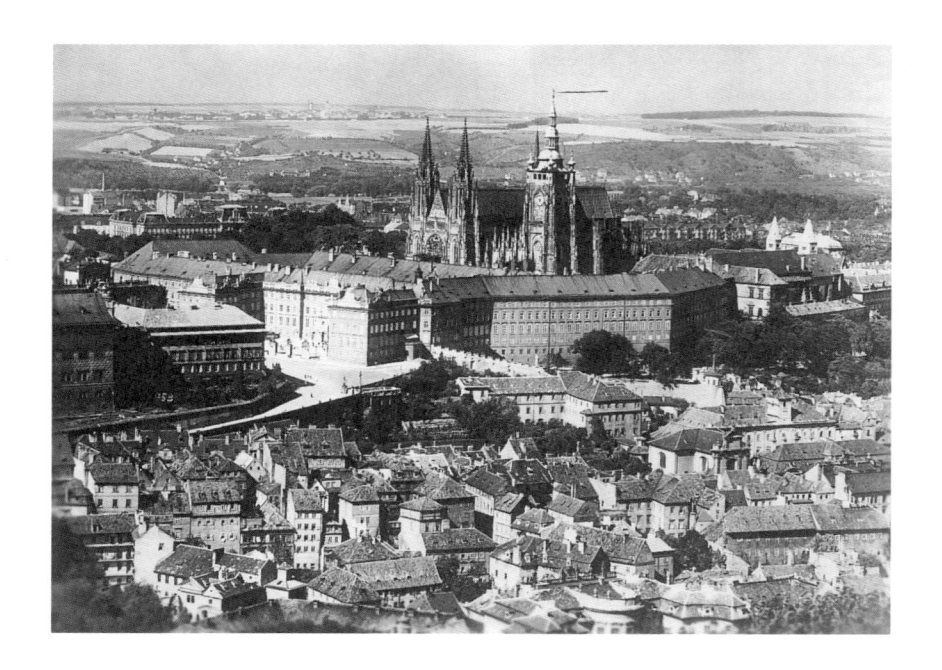

MOZART'S PRAGUE - FACTS

Code for Prague: 02
(international: +42-2-)

MUSEUMS, GRAVES AND MEMORIALS:

BERTRAMKA:
Prague 5, Mozartova 169, phone
02/ 54 38 93 or 55 14 83, fax
53 30 32 (daily 9:30 a.m.–6 p.m.)

ESTATES THEATRE:
Prague 1, Ovocný trh,
phone 24 21 50 01 (rather expensive guided tours can be arranged individually, for advance bookings contact Mrs Pavlíčková)

STRAHOV MONASTERY
(Library)/Strahovská Knihovna:
Prague 1, Strahovské nádvoří 1 (daily 9 a.m.–12 noon and 1 p.m.–5 p.m.), phone 24 51 03 55/407

EVENTS *(a selection; Addresses without phone No.: Advance ticket sale at ticket agencys or the Prague Tourist Centre):*

PRAGUE NATIONAL THEATRE/
NÁRODNÍ DIVADLO (OPERA,
THEATRE, BALLET): Performances –
1) NATIONALTHEATER,
phone 24 91 34 37;
2) STÄNDETHEATER, phone 24 21 50 01

BERTRAMKA
(Chamber music in the Sala terrena or on the terrace from April to Oct.):
Prague 5, Mozartova 169;
Information and bookings
phone 54 38 93, 54 00 12 or
55 14 81-5, fax 53 30 32

ST. NICOLAS CHURCH
(Organ and chamber music concerts):
Prague 1, Staroměstské náměstí,
phone and fax 232 25 89; concerts daily except Monday, start: 6 p.m., Sunday also 3 p.m.; tickets on sale same day in the churches' office from 1 p.m. till concert begins (not to be mistaken for Lesser Side St. Nicolas Church!)

CHURCH OF ST. SIMON AND JUDAS
(Classical concerts): Prague 1, Na Františku, U milosrdných

ST. MARTIN'S CHURCH:
Prague 1, Martinská

CHURCH OF HOLY MARY SNOW:
Prague 1, Jungmannovo náměstí

CHURCH OF OUR SAVIOUR:
Prague 1., Křižovnické náměstí

HAVEL'S CHURCH:
Prague 1., Havelská

LOBKOWITZ PALACE:
Prague 1, Jiřská 3

NOSTITZ PALACE:
Prague 1, Lesser Side, Maltézské náměstí/Malteserplatz 1; tickets c/o Prague concert, phone 24 51 12 85

PALACE CLAM-GALLAS:
Prague 1, Husova 20

PALACE UNITARIA:
Prague 1., Karlova 8

RUDOLFINUM
(Dvořák Hall): Prague 1, Náměstí
Jana Palacha (Mon–Fri 10 a.m.–
12:30 p.m. and 1:30–6 p.m.), phone
24 89 43 27

CLEMENTINUM:
Prague 1, Karlova =
Mariánské náměstí

AGNES CONVENT:
Prague 1, U milosrdných

JACOBS BASILICA AND ABBEY:
Prague 1, Malá Štupartská

BETHLEHEM CHAPEL:
Prague 1, Betlémské náměstí

FRANZ-KAFKA-CENTRE:
Prague 1, Staroměstské náměstí 22/
2nd floor

OPERA MOZART
(Aria medley): Prague 1, Novotného
Lávka 1

NATIONAL PUPPET THEATRE:
Prague 1, Zatecká 1

GENERAL ADVANCE TICKET BOOKING/SALES
(a selection):

BOHEMIA TICKET INTERNATIONAL:
Salvátorská 6 (Mon–Fri 9 a.m.–
12 noon and 1 a.m.–4 p.m., Sat 9 a.m.
–2 p.m.), phone 24 22 78 32; Na
Příkopě 16 (Mon to Fri 9 a.m.–
6 p.m., Sat 9 a.m.–4 p.m., Sun
10 a.m.–3 p.m.), phone 24 21 5031;
Václavské náměstí 27 (Mon–Fri
9 a.m.–6 p.m., Sat 9 a.m.–4 p.m.,
Sun 9 a.m.–2 p.m. (all Prague 1)

HOT LINE
for advance bookings (also for
Groups): phone 232 25 36 or
232 34 29, fax 232 41 89

TOP THEATRE TICKETS:
Celetná 13 or Zatecká or in the Old
Town Hall, Staroměstské náměstí (all
Prague 1)

TICKETPRO:
Laterna Magika, Národni 4 or
Lucerna Stěpánská 61 or Melantrich,
Václavské náměstí,
phone 24 81 40 20 (all Prague 1)

WELL ASSORTED BOOK SHOPS:

KNIHKUPECTVÍ FIŠER:
1, Kaprova 2; phone 2320733

KNIHKUPECTVÍ RŮŽIČKA
(especially for maps and
travel books):
1 Na Příkopě 24;
phone 242 13 037

KNIHKUPECTVÍ BEDNAROVA:
1, Celetná 32; phone 242 0 028

CIZOJAZYČNÉ KNIHKUPECTVÍ
(english spoken):
1, Na Příkopě 27

LYRA PRAGUEENSIS:
1, Karlova 2

CLASSICAL MUSIC CDS:

MUSIC 42:
1, Republiky náměstí 6

MELANTRICH MUSIC STUDIO:
1, Jilská 14

SUPRAPHON:
1, Jungmannova 20

BONTON LAND:
1, Karlova 23

MEGASTORE:
1, Palac Koruna/Václavské náměstí

COFFEE HOUSES:

MALOSTRANSKÁ KAVÁRNA:
Prague 1, Malostranské náměstí 5/28
(daily 9 a.m.–0 p.m.)

KAVÁRNA PRAHA-ROMA:
Prague 1, V jámě 5 (daily 9 a.m.–
10 p.m.)

HOLEŠOVICKÁ KAVÁRNA: Prague 7,
Komunardú 30 (daily 10 a.m.–
12 midnight), phone 80 15 38

DEMÍNKA:
Prague 2, Skrétova 1
(Mon–Fri 9 a.m.–0:30 p.m.),
phone 24 22 33 83

GANY'S:
Prague 1, Národni třida 20 (daily
8 a.m.–0 p.m.), phone 29 76 65.

THE GLOBE:
Prague 7, Janovskeho 14 (daily
10 a.m.–12 midnight),
phone 66 71 2610

VIOLA
(Café and Literature Club): Prague 1,
Národní 7, phone 242 20 844

The legendary
CAFÉ SLAVIA
on Národní will be opening its doors
after years of closure, in late-
autumn 1997. The re-opening of the
renowned COFFEE HOUSE IN THE
TOWN HALL (kavárna, obecní dum)
was in May 1997

**GENERAL TOURIST
INFORMATION:**

CZECH CENTRE FOR TOURISM:
Prague 1, Národní 37 (daily 10 a.m.
–6 p.m.), phone 24 21 14 58

PRAGUE TOURIST CENTRE :
Prague 1, Rytířská 12, phone
24 21 22 09 or 24 23 60 47,
fax 24 21 22 09.
CENTRE FOR BOOKINGS/RESERVATIONS
(Pražská informační služba): 18650
Prague 8, phone 231 0 16,
fax 24 81 61 72

*Warning: in Prague at the moment
opening times, sites for performances
and programmes are frequently
subject to alterations. Also due to
the renewal of the telephone network
telephone numbers may suddenly be
out of date. Therefore, do please
check if neccessary.*

VIENNA

The old Augarten Bridge. Mozart would cross the river here to go to the concerts in the "Alte Favorita".

1 DONAUKANAL/ SCHANZELUFER

(now 1., and 9., Roßauerlände): It is early autumn 1762 and the Mozart family, consisting of Leopold Mozart, his wife Anna, and his children Wolfgang and Nannerl, started its second concert tour to "announce a miracle to the world, born with God's grace in Salzburg" according to Leopold. After the first stop at the Princely court of Passau, the four travellers continued towards the end of September downstream on the Danube to Vienna, arriving in the Imperial City on the 6th October, after stops in Linz, Mauthausen and Ybbs. Their mail-boat "Wasserordinaire" docked on the south shore of the Donaukanal at the so-called Schanzel, near todays Augarten-bridge. It was here where six-year-old Wolfgang set foot on the ground of the city which was to become his adopted home for the last ten years of his life – this major period of creativity between 1781–91.

2 "ZUM WEISSEN OCHSEN"

(Fleischmarkt 28 = Postgasse 11): This former tavern, which belonged to a certain Carl Joseph von Palm, although never mentioned in any contemporary written document, is considered to be the first provisional accomodation of the new arrivals.

3 Palais Collalto

(1., Am Hof 13): This Palais built in 1671 for the Venetian patrician family of the same name, next to the old Jesuit church remodelled by Antonio Carlone, was where Wolfgang and Nannerl performed for the first time, as child prodigies in front of the Viennese public at a private concert, on the evening of the 9th of October 1762.

A few weeks later, on Christmas Day, when the two proffered their skills here a second time, Count Thomas Vinciguerra Collalto distributed the following verse of admiration, composed and printed by himself for the "small six year old pianist from Salzburg" amongst his guests:

The Collalto Palace where six-year-old Wolfgang's first public appearance was made, in concert, for a Viennese audience.

Admirable Child! your virtuosity one praises.
You are so tiny, yet when playing you amaze us
Music holds no strain at all for you, we see.
In no time the greatest Maestro you will be.
My wish for you that body and soul be brave.
End not, like Lübeck's child*, in early grave"

Since 1956 a plaque on the facade of the lovely baroque house has commemorated that memorable first performance.

(* *Reference is made to a six-year-old language genius from Lübeck who created a sensation in his day, but died very young.*)

4 Sites of further appearances made during the first Vienna sojourn: During the autumn of 1762 there were many palaces where Wolfgang and his sister Nannerl were to astonish the aristocracy of the imperial city. More or less verified are accounts of appearances made, amongst others, for Count Johann Joseph WILCZEK (on the 10th October, probably in his city palais, 1., Herrengasse 5); for Count HARRACH (1., Freyung 3); on the 13th for Prince Joseph Maria Friedrich von Sachsen-Hildburghausen in the Palais AUERSPERG (today: 8., Auerspergstraße 1), where a quarter of a century later, in March 1786, a performance of *Idomeneo* was given under the direction of the composer; on the 14th at Countess Maria Theresia KINSKY's Palais (1., Freyung 4); on the

Auersperg Palace, on the street of the same name, was one of many places where the child prodigies, most probably, appeared in concert.

VIENNA

The summer residence of Maria Theresia, as seen from the garden side. The Palace of Schönbrunn, painted by Bernado Bellotto, called Canaletto, c. 1760.

16th for Count PÁLFFY (1., Josefsplatz 6); on the 17th for Count Franz Thun-Valsassina (probably in the PASSAUERHOF, 1., Salzgries 21 = Passauerplatz 6) and on the 9th of November at the HOUSE OF THE WINDISCHGRAETZ (today: 1., Bankgasse 7) for Marchioness Vincenzia Pacheco.

5 SCHÖNBRUNN PALACE (13., Schönbrunner Schloßstrasse): One week after their arrival, in the afternoon of 13. October, much to the joy of the career-minded father, the first concert by the child prodigies was given at the Imperial Court. In all probability the Great Gallery, a reminder of the mirrored hall in the Palace of Versailles, was where the musical reception took place. In attendance, amongst others, were Maria Theresia and her consort Franz Stephan, Archduchess Marie-Antoinette and the court composer Georg Christoph Wagenseil. Leopold proudly reported to his friend Hagenauer in Salzburg, "… we were so graciously received by their Majesties that if I were to relate this, one would think my tale a fable. Enough! Wolferl (little Wolfgang) jumped up onto the Empress's lap, hugged her and kissed her thoroughly. In a word, we were there with her from 3 to 6 p.m. and the Emperor came out himself to call me into the other room to hear the Archduchess play the violin …"

Two days later the imperial couple showed their appreciation by sending two gala dresses, which were

Renovated more than once, and visited every year by more and more people. Nevertheless, Schönbrunn Palace, seen here from the "courtyard of honour" side, has hardly changed since Mozart's time.

VIENNA

W. A. Mozart as a child. Dressed in the court attire given to him by Empress Maria Theresia. Wherever he performed in concert the reaction of the nobility was overwhelming. The painting is thought to be the work of Pietro Antonio Lorenzoni, 1763.

to be delivered by their paymaster, to Wolfgang and Nannerl. The Mozarts returned to the Palace on the 16th to visit Maria Theresia's youngest children, the Archdukes Ferdinand and Maximilian. And on the 21st they enjoyed the honour of a second reception with the two "Serenest of Majesties".

The summer residence of the Hapsburgs did not focus in Mozart's creative life again until 1786: On the 7th of February that same year it was in the Orangerie – the 190m long, 11m wide, 8m high green-house adapted in 1994/95 for performances and exhibitions – where the first performance of *Der Schauspieldirektor (K 486)* was given in honour of Duke Albert of Saxony and his wife, Archduchess Marie Christine.

6 Tiefer Graben 20

(1., Apartment house): About two weeks later, around the 20th of October, the Mozart family moved from the "Weißen Ochsen" (White Ox) into the socalled "Tischler-Haus". The room on the first floor was, lamented Leopold Mozart in a letter to his friend Lorenz Hagenauer, "1000 paces long and 1 pace wide". Nevertheless the room was kept till the end of December when the return journey was made to Salzburg. The historic house was demolished long ago, but is often mistaken in written sources for the old building still standing at No.16.

Mozart frequently moved to the Tiefer Graben. The picture shows the view from the Tiefer Graben up to the Wipplingerstraße, painted by Franz Alt, 1843.

VIENNA

7 GARIBOLDISCHES HOUSE
(1., Weihburggasse 3): It was on the occasion of the wedding of Archduchess Maria Josepha Gabriela, Maria Theresia's ninth daughter, to Ferdinand IV, the last King of Naples-Sicily, mid-September 1767, when Mozart's father, together with his wife, the eleven year old Mozart and his sister returned to Vienna. Lodgings were taken for three weeks with the goldsmith Gottfried Johann Schmalecker, on the second floor of the so-called "Gariboldisches Haus" (once Stadt/City No. 938, today No. 3). The building continued to serve as an elegant hotel during the 19th century, where, amongst others, Franz Liszt, Richard Wagner and Anton Bruckner resided.

8 APARTMENT HOUSE
(1., Concordiaplatz 1–4 = Salzgrieß 18): The building previously found at this address was where the Mozarts stayed temporarily in October 1767.

9 MESMER-HOUSE AND GARDEN
(3., Rasumofskygasse 29): Dr. Franz Anton Mesmer, a versatile and talented physician from the Bodensee region, today considered one of the pioneers of psychotherapy due to the curative method of "mesmeric magnetizing" that he developed, was a great lover of music, and as such a close friend of the Mozart's. His magnificent premises in the Rauchfangkehrergasse (today Rasumofskygasse) in the suburbs of Landstrasse served the Morart family as a centrally-located place to meet the Viennese society. It was here, in autumn 1768, where the twelve-year-old's first musical comedy *Bastien und Bastienne*, was performed for the first time. In the summer of 1773 Mozart's father mentions in his correspondance "a great music" – in Mesmer's garden – a vast Rococo park that he praises as "incomparable with its statues, theatre, avery, dove-cote and on the hill a belvedere".

10 TAVERN "ZUM ROTEN SÄBEL"
(The Red Sabel) (Wipplingerstraße 19 = Färbergasse 5): After returning from Olomouc in early January 1768, where both children had suffered from

VIENNA

A ball in the Hofburg, the Hapsburg's winter palace. Mozart loved to dance and was often to take part in the socalled "Redoutes". Aquarelle drawing by Joseph Schütz.

smallpox, the Mozart family took lodgings in the tavern named "Grünwaldisches Haus". They were to stay here for almost one whole year. During this time Wolfgang composed, amongst other works, *two symphonies in D major (K 45 and 48)* as well as the *Mass in C minor (K 139)* which became known as the *Waisenhausmesse* (Orphanage Mass).

11 HOFBURG (WIEN 1.,):
On the 19th of January the Mozarts were received by Empress Maria Theresia and her son Joseph in the Leopold-wing of the Hapsburg residence, and Leopold later proudly relates, treated "with utmost intimacy".

Thirteen years later, in Autumn 1781, Wolfgang gave a concert in honour of Prince Württemberg in the Swiss-wing of the Palace. He also attended many festivities and masked balls in the Redouten halls. His operas were to be performed here repeatedly (see Hofbibliothek, 39).

A wing of the Vienna Hofburg Palace, where the Mozarts were graciously received by Emperor and Empress.

12 WAISENHAUSKIRCHE "MARIA GEBURT" (Orphanage Church) (3., Rennweg near 91): In 1759 the Empress had appointed a certain Father Prahammer as administrator of the "Waisenhaus", an extensive housing and school block for orphaned pupils.

For the occasion of the consecration of the new church, a Classisistic building by Thaddäus Karner,

This church on the Rennweg was where Mozart's *Waisenhausmesse* was performed for the first time.

The commemorative plaque on the facade of the Waisenhauskirche (= Orphanage Church).

(the foundation stone had been laid by Joseph II three years earlier), Mozart had composed "a solemn Mass, an Oratorium and a trumpet concert which he dedicated to the orphanage". All three works were heard for the first time on the 7th of December 1768, in the presence of the Empress Maria Theresia.

The Vienna newspaper "Wienerische Diarium" reported, "… with general applause and admiration, performed by Mozart himself, conducted with greatest accuracy".

13 APARTMENT HOUSE

(1., Tiefer Graben 18): This house, built in 1764 (exterior alterations in 1840), belonged to a copper-smith named Gottlieb Friedrich Fischer. It was here, where Mozart father and son stayed during their third sojourn mid-June to mid-September 1773. Whilst Wolfgang waited impatiently – in vain – for an appointment at court, he composed, among other works, *six string quartets (K 168–173), one serenade* and *one march in D major(K 185 and 189)* and choral music for *Thamos, König in Ägypten.* Since 1941 the facade has been adorned with a memorial plaque carrying a rather strange inscription "Vienna's music experience determined here the path of the master of German Art"?

14 JESUITENKIRCHE

(Church of the Jesuits) (1., Am Hof): On the 8th of August 1773, just a month before the Jesuit order was dissolved and the church "Am Hof" was given to the Vienna garrison, Leopold Mozart conducted his son's *Domenicus Messe (C major, K 66)* here. This was where two of Wolfgang and Constanze's children, Raimund Leopold and Anna, were to receive the holy sacrament of baptism in 1783 and 1789 (both died in infancy). From the balcony of this same church in April 1782 Pope Pius VI gave his blessing to the people of Vienna.

Easter 1782, Am Hof, Pope Pius VI blesses the people of Vienna, from the balcony of the former Jesuit Church. Coloured copper engraving by Carl Schütz, 1782.

The magnificent Baroque facade of the church, seen here, is the work of Carlo Antonio Carlone, 1662.

15 ARTARIA & CO.

(today: 1., Kohlmarkt 18): In the three-story corner building "Zu den drei Laufern" (to the three runners) in the immediate vicinity of St. Michael's Church (not to be mistaken for the Artaria-House built by Max Fabiani around 1900 at 9!) the well known publishing firm "Artaria & Co", that published many of Mozarts works in his time, had its business premises.

16 "HAUS DES DEUTSCHEN RITTERORDENS" (House of the Teutonic Knights) (Singerstraße 7 = Stephansplatz 4): It was in March 1781 when Wolfgang Amadeus finally obeyed the orders of his employer, Prince-Archbishop Hieronymus Colleredo, to follow him from Munich to Vienna. Here at the Archbishop's residence, an extensive place, built around two impressive inner-courtyards, he was expected, as "Kapellmeister" of the Salzburg court orchestra, to live with the whole entourage, which meant under supervision, and to participate in the numerous concerts that were held. It was here in May of the same year, when he resigned his post to try his luck as a free-lance musician in the Imperial City, where it came to the legendary scene: Count Arco, responsible not only for catering but also for music, had the insubordinate subject "kicked in the pants and sent packing". Whereupon Mozart, after his dismissal, wrote to his father on the 9th of May: "... I will hear no more of Salzburg – I hate the Archbishop to madness." The writing on the commemorative plaque at the entrance to Singerstraße states that Mozart stayed here from 16th March to the 2nd May 1781.

Wooden verandas in the beautifully renovated inner courtyard, home to the Order of the Teutonic Knights.

17 KÄRNTNERTOR-THEATER

(1., Philharmoniker-/Kärntner Straße/ Albertinaplatz): "... Yesterday I was quite pleased with the Viennese public. I played at the Widows Concert in the Kärntnerthor Theatre and had to begin all over again, as the applause was never ending ..." What Mozart was so enthused about was his first appearance, the evening before, at a benefit performance in aid of the widows and orphans of musicians for the

VIENNA

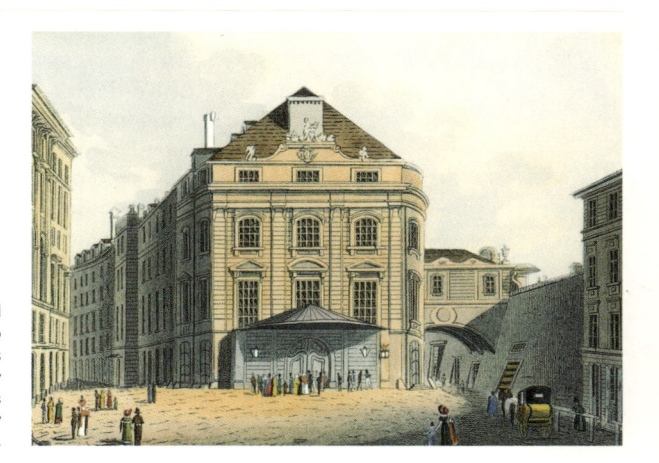

The "Royal and Imperial Court Theatre next to the Kärntner Gate" was one of the leading play houses in Mozart's Vienna. Engraving by Tranquillo Mollo, c. 1825.

The auditorium of the theatre, five floors, boxes all the way round, opened in 1763. Engraving by Tranquillo Mollo, c. 1825.

Vienna Musicians' Society. This institution was established in 1771 following the example of a similar one in London. The above mentioned Kärntnertor-Theater, a five story building that was to be demolished only after the inauguration of the new Court Opera House (1869), opened its doors for the first time in 1763. It would have been located roughly where the Hotel Sacher stands today, and served, like the old Burgtheater, as a place for concert performances. Mozart frequently played and conducted his works here.

Cäcilia Weber, mother of Constanze and Aloisia.

18 Apartment House "Zum Auge Gottes"
(1., Milchgase 1/Petersplatz 11/Tuchlauben 8): "In this house Mozart lived and composed his 'Entführung aus dem Serail' (*Abduction from the Seraglio*). What the memorial plaque does not say, is: that the original two-part edifice gave way to the big Gründerzeit building of today in 1897; that the recently dismissed free-lancer much against the will of his father, found lodgings here as Cäcilia Weber's tenant, her second eldest, meanwhile married daughter Aloisia had years before been Mozart's first great love, and that the 25-year-old was about to fall in love with her one year younger, as yet unmarried sister, Constanze; and that in the "pretty room on the 2nd floor" firstly only parts of the Turkish-musical comedy featuring Belmonte, Konstanze, Bassa Selim and Osmin and, secondly, amongst others a number of *violin sonatas (K 376/377 and 379/380)* as well as the rest of the *wind-serenade in E major, the Gran Partita, (K 361)* were created.

19 Cobenzl
(19., Am Cobenzl 98): In the summer of 1781 Mozart received an invitation from State Chancellor Johann Philip Count Cobenzl to spend some days in July at his country estate on the so-called Reisenberg. Mozart wrote the following about the landscape on

Count Cobenzl's park on the Reisenberg. There was a wonderful panorama view of Vienna from here.
Etching from Joh. Ziegler, copied from Laurenz Janscha, c. 1800.

VIENNA

Around 1800 Fanny von Arnstein, née Itzig, was the Grande Dame of the Viennese social and cultural life. Vinzenz Kininger copied the demitint portrait from an original by Jean Urbain Guerin, 1804.

today's Höhenstraße near the Kahlenberg: "It is an hour away from Vienna ... The house is nothing, but the surroundings, the forest, in which he (Count Cobenzl) built a Grotto, as if it were from nature's own hand, it is splendid and most agreeable ..."

20 APARTMENT HOUSE
(1., Graben 17): On May 2nd 1781 Wolfgang had moved to the Webers house in the Milchgasse (see: 18 Apartment House). But in late-summer "because of people gossiping" he had moved to the representative address at the corner of Graben-Habsburgergasse. His room on the third floor was fairly frugal. It was, he wrote to his father, "so full with the wardrobe, table and piano that I would not know where one could put a bed".

Nevertheless he lived here until shortly before his wedding to Constanze in summer 1782. Whilst he stayed at this residence, his first important female

The Flour Market with Schwarzenberg Palace in the background. An aquarelle by Rudolf von Alt, 1838.

piano-students came here for lessons, and he composed, along side numerous smaller pieces, the *Haffner-Symphony (D major, K 385)*. The man who rented out the rooms in the splendid four-story building, which was the only representative address in the city at that time that any Jew could hold as an independant landlord and sublet (before the "Toleranz Patent", Emperor Joseph's freedom act), was the court actor Adam Isaac Arnstein. He kept a house-hold of over thirty people! It is not known, as there are no records, whether or not Mozart was better aquainted with the man's son, the banker Nathan Adam Arnstein whose wife Fanny, neé Itzig, was later to rise to become one of the most scintillating key-figures in Vienna's high society. Whatever the case, both names did appear on the lists of Mozart's subscription concerts. The subsequent building to the "Arnstein House" today, which is by no means small either, dates back to 1905.

▢ 21 Tavern "Zur Mehlgrube"
(1., Neuer Markt 5 = Kärntner Straße 22): Opposite the Capuchin Church on Neuer Markt, about where the luxury Hotel Ambassador stands today, there was a tavern already in existence from about the end of the 17th century. It was called "Zur Mehlgrube" (to the Flour Pit) – referring to the citys flour warehouse which had once stood on the very same spot.

Tickets like these were much sought after – for a number of years – by the Viennese society.

Already in Mozart's day grand balls and concerts were held here, due to the lack of other adequate localities and because this tavern had an astonishingly splendid hall. During the ball season 1781/82 a business man, Philipp Jakob Martin, had, with the Emperor's permission, begun to organise regular "Amateur Concerts", to which high-class performers often came and performed. Among them Mozart, who at the beginning of 1785, arranged a cycle of a total of six subscription concerts, and made a personal appearance himself as a pianist, like on the 11th February when his *piano concerto in D major (K 466)* was to be heard for the first time.

22 "Alte Favorita"

(2., Obere Augartenstraße 1): Another popular meeting point for the musically-minded Viennese public was at the "matineé concerts" in the Augarten, to be exact, in the building complex named "Alte Favorita", which today serves as home to the legendary Augarten porcelain manufacturers. Joseph II had opened the gates

Gottfried Bernhard Baron van Swieten. Copper engraving by Joh. Ernst Mansfeld, c. 1780.

Where, today, porcelain is manufactured and the Vienna Boys Choir practice, Mozart once played.

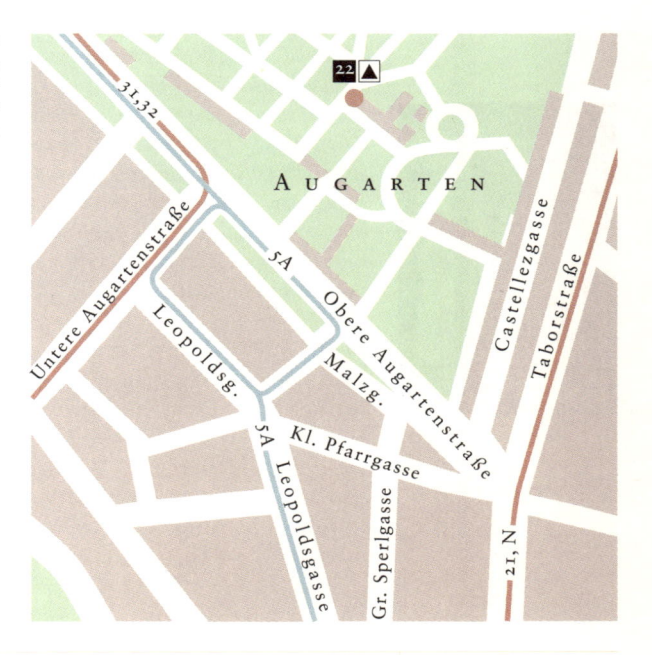

VIENNA

The entrance to the Augarten, where the building complex "Alte Favorita" was located. Coloured copper engraving by Joh. Ziegler, c. 1800.

of the roughly half a million square meters of park to his relaxation and recreation seeking subjects. In no time at all the above mentioned Philipp Jakob Martin went into action. The concerts were held in the restaurant of the court culinarian and cook, Ignaz Jahn (see: 37 Jahnscher Saal).

Extremely popular on warm summer evenings were the serenade performances, which were known under the strange name of "lemonade sheds". Here as well, Mozart organised his own concerts entirely at his own financial risk, which was a perfectly normal occurance in those days. But they were not quite as successful as he had hoped they would be. The first concert was staged on the 26th May 1782. Mozart was to perform a symphony by Gottfried van Swieten and then his own *E major concert for two pianos (K 365)*.

On the side wall of the building there is a memorial plaque which acts as a reminder that, here inside, not only Mozart, but also Beethoven and Schubert appeared in concert.

The interior of St. Stephan's Cathedral. Mozart and Constanze were married here in August 1782. Engraving by Traquillo Mollo, c. 1825.

23 ST. STEPHAN'S CATHEDRAL (1., Stephansplatz): According to the register "the very noble Mr. Wolfgang Adam (sic) Mozart and the very noble J. Konstantia Weberin" were married on the 4th August 1782 in the Cathedral and Metropolitan Church of St. Stephan, (without Leopold's blessing, as he was strictly against his son marrying "a Weber"). In the same church two of their children, Johann Thomas Leopold and Franz Xaver Wolfgang, were christened. And on the 6th December

VIENNA

1791 Mozart's corpse was given its last blessing in the "Crucifix Chapel of the new Crypt", on the northern side of the Albertinian choir next to the Capistran pulpit (the memorial plaque can be seen from outside). Earlier that same year on the 9th May the city council had generously given him the "appointment of assistant to the Domkapellmeister", an – unpaid! – position which he had personally requested.

24 APARTMENT HOUSE
(1., Wipplingersraße 14): After spending a few months, from July till December 1782, in the "Roten Säbel" (he had stayed here once before, see: 10 Zum roten Säbel), he moved to this address just a few houses further down the street, now in the company of his newly wedded wife. "We are staying", he wrote to his father in Salzburg, "... on the hohen Brücke ... in the small Herberstein house No. 412 on the 3rd floor, with Herr von Wetzlar, a rich Jew. Well, I have a room which is 1000 paces long and one pace wide, a bedroom then a hall and a nice big kitchen". The original building no longer exists today, the present one dates back to 1860.

25 APARTMENT HOUSE
(1., Kohlmarkt 7): Already in February 1783 the married couple were to change their address. The reason: Because of the financial difficulties they were experiencing,

St. Stephan's Cathedral. A Gothic achievement, built with 20 000 cub.m of sandstone.

A view of the Judenplatz. Engraving copied from a painting by Salomon Kleiner, 1725.

and for the sake of their landlord Wetzlar who had not charged them any rent, they had been obliged to leave. Their new home, an old inner-city house, was, as Mozart documented in a letter, "an awful abode". He did not have to suffer very long.

26 APARTMENT HOUSE

(1., Judenplatz 3 = Kurrentgasse 5): Mozart's sixth home in the two years that he had been in Vienna was to be, only three months later, in April of 1783, the "Burgish House" No. 244 on the Judenplatz. In these "good quarters", he stayed until December. Wolfgangs first son, Raimund Leopold was born here on the 17th June, but died only a few months later of the notorious bowel sickness. Both this and the neighbouring building (see: 39 apartment house), which was the more important of the two for Mozarts biography, were demolished before 1900.

27 TRATTNERHOF

(1., Graben 29–29a): In January 1784 a further move was organized. The new address: an apartment in the second stairwell on the third floor of the Trattnerhof on the Graben, one of the biggest and most prestigious tenement houses during the era of Josephinism in Vienna. It belonged to the entrepreneur

VIENNA

Johann Thomas Edler von Trattner, court- book dealer and printer. The preceding block – today's building was re-built in 1911/12 by Rudolf Krauß – was in today's sense multi-functional. Besides apartments, in which about 600 people lived, there were many business premises and a large hall, where Mozart held three highly successful subscription concerts in the second half of March, performing his three *piano concertos* (K 449–451) for the first time.

Shortly before moving yet again, his second son, Carl Thomas, was born here on the 21st of September 1784. The Trattners were to act as his God-parents, as they were for three more of Mozart's children.

28 PETERS CHURCH

(1., Petersplatz): In this church, a splendid example of high-Baroque period in Austria, two of the Mozart's children were baptised, Carl Thomas (1784–1858) and Theresia (1787–1788).

One of the big building sites in the Vienna of Joseph II: the Trattnerhof on the Graben. Etching by Friedrich August Brand, c. 1775.

One of Austria's finest examples of high-Baroque architecture: St. Peter's Church. Designed by Gabriele Montani, Andre Altomonte and probably J. L. von Hildebrandt. Engraving by Tranquillo Mollo, c. 1825.

133 VIENNA

29 "Figaro House"
(1., Domgasse 5 = Schulerstraße 8):
In this five-story building, located in the immediate vicinity of St. Stephan's Cathedral, Constanze and Wolfgang Amadeus spent two and a half happy and successful years – from September 1784 to April 1787. The piano nobile (principle floor) with its original door, the old floor made of spruce-wood planks, panelling, and window sills from the late-Rococo period is the only surviving Mozart-apartment and as such a memorial of major importance.

The building known as "The Figaro House" received its present-day appearance at the beginning of the 18th century through the owner and master builder Andrea Simone Carove. He had also been responsible for, among other buildings, Prince Eugene's magnificent winter palace in the Himmelpfortgasse. Carove's son-in-law was the highly regarded court stucco supplier Albert Camesina, who took over the house after him and is the one to thank for the splendid chamber on the first floor with the well preserved, beautiful, grey-pink stucco-reliefs, in which Mozart's very own composers desk was soon to stand.

For this noble home, consisting of four rooms, two small chambers and some small side rooms, Mozart paid the stately sum of 480 guilders in rent. This was where a number of important works were created – among others the *masonic mourning music*, the cantata

The Domgasse is just as medieval as it was when Mozart lived there.

Domgasse No. 5 – a must for Mozart-lovers from all over the world. This was where *"Le nozze di Figaro"* and other important works were composed.

VIENNA

134

Davidde penitente, eleven *piano concertos*, one for *horn*, two *quintets*, three *trios*, *string quartets* dedicated to Haydn, many *piano sonatas*, the Goethe-Lied *Das Veilchen* (*the Violet*) available at the Museum entrance as a facsimile, and last but not least, the *Marriage of Figaro* (*K 492*). Constanze gave birth to Johann Thomas Leopold here on the 18th October 1786, but the baby lived for less than a month.

The Mozarts often received guests here: Joseph Haydn for example. In the spring of 1785 Leopold Mozart stayed for some weeks, and in the second week of April 1787, in all probability, so did the sixteen-year-old Ludwig van Beethoven. Johann Nepomuk Hummel, a musically highly-talented seven-year-old boy, was to stay with Mozart for two years. And decades later the young Johannes Brahms, a new arrival to the city, was to find his way here as well.

Consecrated in such a way the premises were to be refurbished as an apartment in 1941, adapted as a museum fifteen years later and then in 1991, the bicentennial year of Mozart's death, completely renovated and rearranged. In the altogether seven rooms – drawing-room, bedroom and guest-rooms, former kitchen and Mozart's study – there are many interesting documents relating to his person, his works and his social environment (a detailed catalogue is on sale at the entrance to the apartment). There is a special audio-treat availabe to the visitor: Listening in to the various musical excerpts that are played over the earphones.

Johann Wolfgang von Goethe, 14-years of age, saw Mozart, the child prodigy, perform in Frankfurt.

🔵 30 LODGE "ZUR NEUGEKRÖNTEN HOFFNUNG" (Newly crowned hope) (1., Landskrongasse 1 = Wildpretmarkt 10): On the 14th of December 1784 Mozart ceremoniously entered the Freemason Lodge "Zur Wohltätigkeit" (to charity) – it was in the house on the Marc-Aurel-Straße 5 (Vorlaufstraße 2) – and three weeks later, on January the 7th 1785, was promoted to the rank of Fellow Craft. Shortly afterwards, according to the new charter of 1785, various Lodges were to be united under the title of "Zur neugekrönten Hoffnung" (Newly crowned hope). This Lodge had its seat in the inner city house No. 563 that belonged to a

Mozart and a Freemason brother, probably Emanuel Schikaneder. Detail from the picture on the opposite page.

"Freemason Lodge in Vienna" (artist unknown, c. 1780/90). The picture shows the Brotherhood during an initiation ritual.

Copper engraving by Ignaz Alberti, 1791, showing many Freemason symbols from the first text book for *The Magic Flute*.

certain Baron Moser, and once stood at the above address before the new building of today. As member and "house composer" of the newly established Lodge Mozart wrote two choral pieces, one for the ceremony of the inauguration on January 14th 1786 the *Zur Eröffnung der Loge (Opening of the Lodge) (K 483)* and one for the *Zum Schluß der Loge (Retiring of the Lodge) (K 484)*. In addition to the two works for the Lodge mentioned above, he also composed in these months, the cantata *Die Maurerfreude (Masonic Joy) (K 471)* and the *Mauerische Trauermusik (Masonic Funeral Music) (K 477)*.

▲ 31 ALTES BURGTHEATER
(1., Michaelerplatz; today: Michaelertor or -wing): In 1776 Emperor Joseph II ordered the "Theater nächst der Burg", which stood approximately where today the Michaelertor leads from the square of the same name through to the Hofburg, to be elevated to the rank of "Royal and Imperial Court and National Theatre". It was the rulers intention to ethically and morally educate his subjects in opinion and taste. Today's Burgtheater on the Lueger-Ring, built by Semper and Hasenauer, took over this function more than a hundred years later.

The "Alte Burgtheater" (a middle-sized building of 44 m in length, 15 m wide and with room for an audience of 1360) played a major role in promulgating the works of Mozart. Three of his operas were performed here for the first time ever – the *Abduction* (on the 16th July 1782), *Le Nozze di Figaro* (on the 1st of May 1786) and *Così fan tutte* (on the 26th January 1790) – and four more were played here on Viennese soil for the first time. Mozart was to appear frequently in this house as soloist and conductor at music concerts. About one especially successful concert on the evening of the 23rd March 1783, he wrote: "The theatre could not possibly have been any fuller, all the seats in the boxes were taken. – but the dearest thing for me though was, that his majesty, the Emperor, was present. How delighted he was and how loud his applause was for me!"

Detail of a title-page from the first printing of the piano score from *Così fan tutte* (1785).

32 Casino

(2., Untere Donaustraße 5): In the so-called Freemason-Casino, in the long since demolished coffee-house Mayer in the Leopoldstadt, in Advent in the year 1786, Mozart arranged a cycle of four concerts. Among other pieces it was here that the *piano concerto in C major (K 503)* was performed for the first time – the climax and end of that series of twelve "great" piano concertos he had composed in just three years between 1784 and 1786.

On this engraving by Tranquillo Mollo, c. 1825, the Royal and Imperial National Theatre can still be seen on the Michaelerplatz.

"View towards Landstraße" – Mozart lived in this suburb for a while. This was where his friend, Messmer, had a home. Copper engraving by Joh. Ziegler, 1780.

33 APARTMENT HOUSE

(3., Landstraßer Hauptstraße 75–77): At the end of April 1787 the Mozarts left their quarters in the Domgasse, after what had for them been an unusually long and settled period of two and a half years. As far as the reasons for this change of address were concerned, even Leopold could only guess, as he wrote to his daughter: "… he lives now on the Landstraße No. 224. Though he gives no reason for it. Nothing! this unfortunately I must guess." The new home was in the garden wing of a suburban house in rural surroundings, (the original has in the meantime been replaced by a new building). The apartment was, to say the least, rather modest and according to the "Josephinischen Steuerfassion"(tax laws of the Josephine era) of those days, consisted of: a room, closet, small chamber, kitchen, pantry, wood store-room and attic. Mozart was at this time experiencing enormous financial difficulties. The eight months spent here brought forth among the main pieces, the *Kleine Nachtmusik* (a little night music) *(K 525)*, the *violin sonata* in *A major (K 526)* and, especially, a substantial part of *Don Giovanni (K 527)*. At this time he also became much better acquainted with the family of the botanist, Nikolaus Joseph von Jacquin, who lived in the nearby Rennweg.

34 APARTMENT HOUSE

(1., Tuchlauben = Schultergasse 2): These lodgings, where the Mozarts stayed from December 1787 to mid-June the following year, appear in the biography, more than anything else, as the birthplace

VIENNA

of their first daughter Theresia Konstanzia Adelheid, who died in infancy. At this time Mozart's star as a concert arranger and piano virtuoso began to fade. In spite of this, here in the Tuchlauben, in these quite unimpressive surroundings, (there's a large apartment house from the Gründerzeit there today) he composed, apart from many smaller pieces, the *piano concerto in D major (K 537)* better known as the *Krönungskonzert (Coronation Concerto)*.

35 STARHEMBERGSCHES HOUSE
(1., Dorotheergasse 9): In later days Mozart's public appearances were rare. One of them that took place here is recorded, thanks to a diary note made by Count Zinzendorf: At the beginning of February 1788 he played for the Venetian envoy, Andrea Dolfin.

36 APARTMENT HOUSE
(1., Währinger Straße 26): After moving from their lodgings in the suburb of Landstraße on June 17th 1788 the Mozarts went to live yet again outside the city walls/bastion. This – like so many other houses

Mozart's very own writing, the andante, the beginning of the *Jupiter* symphony (K 551).

no longer in existence – was called "Zu den drei Sternen" (to the three stars) and was, most probably, not what one would have called representative. Its great advantage, according to Mozart, was: the garden, in which one could compose in peace. The results of this creative phase of non-disturbance were, along side smaller chamber-music pieces, the *Divertimento (K 563)*, the three great *symphonies* in *E major (K 543)*, *G minor (K 550)* and the *Jupiter* in *C major (K 551)* and not to forget the famous *canons (K 553–562)*. Especially the one with the incomparable title *Bona nox! bist a rechta Ox* (Good night! You are an Ox, all right.)

▲ 37 JAHNSCHER SAAL
(1., Himmelpfortgasse 6): On the first floor of this former burghers house, above today's Café Frauenhuber, Ignaz Jahn (this was the cook and court culinarian already mentioned in connection with concerts in the Augarten, see: 22 "Alte Favorita") held a number of much appraised concerts at the end of the 18th century. The commemorative plaque visible on the facade of the house records that Mozart was actively, personally involved in these performances. It was here in November of 1788, in the hall with room for an audience of about 400 people, that his adaption of Händel's pastorale "Acis and Galatea" *(K 566)* was heard. And on the 4th March 1791, his last public appearance as a pianist, he played his *piano concerto* in *B major (K 595)* for the first time. By the way, at this

The National Library on Josephsplatz. In the Grand Hall Mozart often swung the conducters baton. Engraving by Tranquillo Mollo, c. 1825.

VIENNA

moment in time, Aloisia Weber, Mozart's sister-in-law and first real love, was staying just a few paces further down the road, at Himmelpfortgasse 11. She had, in the meantime, married the artist Joseph Lange and was enjoying success as a singer.

38 Hofbibliothek

(Court Library) (1., Josefsplatz 1): Gottfried Freiherr van Swieten, an active friend and promoter of music and the son of Maria Theresia's personal physician, had founded the Society of Cavaliers in 1786 for representatives of the high ranking aristocracy. The aim was to foster the great oratories by Händel and Haydn. As prefect of the court library since 1777, he was often to organize respective performances in the library's grand hall. Mozart arranged and adapted many of Händel's choral and orchestra works for these occasions, e. g. the pastorale "Acis and Galatea" *(K 566)*. From 1788 on, beneath the magnificent ceiling fresco by Daniel Gran, he frequently conducted the performances himself. Known as the National Library today and open at certain hours to visitors, this shrine for book-lovers was begun under the reign of Charles VI by Johann Bernhard Fischer von Erlach and finished by his son Joseph Emanuel.

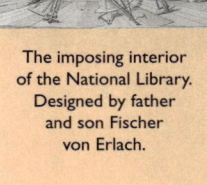

The imposing interior of the National Library. Designed by father and son Fischer von Erlach.

39 Apartment House

(1., Judenplatz 4): The house known as "Zur Mutter Gottes" (to the Mother of God) which like its neighbouring house (see: 26 Apartment House) has long since been demolished, was where Mozart stayed from January 1789 till September 1790 (he had stayed here once before in 1783). Apparently, after a while, the distance from his home in Währing to the city had proved too much of a hindrance.

In this somewhat modest abode, during the winter of 1789/90, he composed among other works the *quintet for clarinet* in *A major (K 581)* for his friend Anton Paul Stadler and the opera *Così fan tutte* which was performed for the first time at the end of January 1790 in the Burgtheater. For the purpose of rehearsing *Così fan tutte* he invited his masonic brothers, his ever-

The clarinetist and friend of Mozart, Anton Paul Stadler.

Hohe Markt, where Mozart's benefactor, Johann Michael Puchberg lived. Lithography by X. Sandmann.

Ground plan of the, no longer existing, house in the Rauhensteingasse where Mozart died. Aquarelle drawing by Emil Hütter, 1806.

patient creditor Johann Michael Puchberg and his "dearest" fatherly friend and admired admirer Joseph Haydn to his home on New Year's Eve Day.

40 APARTMENT HOUSE
(1., Hoher Markt 1): The owner of this house was Franz Count Walsegg-Stuppach. This was the man who became famous under rather strange circumstances after commissioning the *Requiem*. It was Johann Michael Puchberg who had an apartment here, and where Constanze Mozart was to stay for a period between April and June 1789 whilst her husband was on his Berlin tour.

41 APARTMENT HOUSE
(1., Rauhensteingasse 8 = Kärntner Straße 19; today: department store "Steffl"): On the 30th September 1790 Constanze moved from the Judenplatz to this place, the so-called "Kleine Kayserhaus", while her husband was still in Frankfurt. In the piano nobile of the fine middle-class house Mozart was to compose, after his return, his last great works: amongst others the *B major piano concerto (K 595)*, the *E major string quintett (K 614)*, *the concert for klarinet* in *A major (K 622)*, *the Freemason cantata (K 623)*, parts of the *Magic Flute (K 620)* and, after a strange anonymous messenger had brought him the

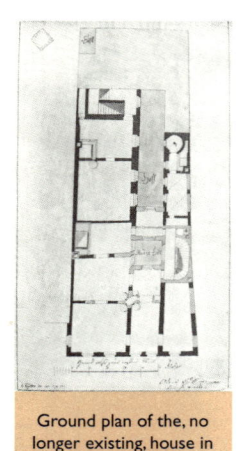

VIENNA

order, a major part of the *Requiem (K 626)*, which was later completed by Franz Xaver Süßmayr. Here Constanze was to give birth to their last son, Franz Xaver, on 26th July 1791. At fifty five minutes after midnight on the 5th December – the doctor had just bled him, given him vomiting powder and applied cold compresses – Mozart passed away after two weeks of suffering. "Hitziges Frieselfieber" (hot shivering fevers) was the official reason for his death, as subsequently documented in the St. Stephan's parish death records. A violent bout of rheumatic fever – or, as a result, heart failure –, as experts later diagnosed.

The original house was demolished in the middle of the last century. The building that was erected instead, the "Mozarthof", was to be replaced almost entirely in the 1960's by a department store named Steffl. In the music department there are some reminders and

Mozart's snuff-box. Many precious gifts, like the one in the picture, were given to him by the wealthy concert goer.

The house where Mozart died in the Rauhensteingasse. Today the far less attractive department store stands in its place. Aquarelle by Emil Hütter, 1847.

VIENNA

Scene from a historical performance of *The Magic Flute*. Tamino plays the flute, taming even the wildest of animals.

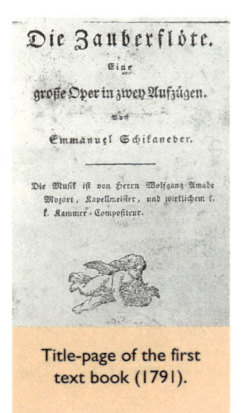

Title-page of the first text book (1791).

Emanuel Schikaneder. Stipple etching by Philipp Richter, c.1810

facsimile with explanatory texts, and at the back of the house, in the Rauhensteingasse, there is a memorial plaque that was donated by the Society of the Friends of Music in 1927. For the coming years the owners of the building have plans to generally refurbish the whole place, during the course of which, it has been indicated, the room where Mozart died will be reconstructed.

42 Theatre im Freihaus

(4., Wiedner Hauptstraße 10/Margaretenstraße 10–16/Operngasse 25): Towards the end of the 18th century in the suburb of Wieden, near the city, between the above named streets, there was the so-called Freihaus; an extensive block of countless tenement flats, with 32 stairways and six courtyards, belonging to Prince Starhemberg. In 1785 in the sixth courtyard the "Theatre on the Wieden" alias "Freihaus" was erected – a stone, tile-covered building, modest in size: 30 × 15 m and with a 10 × 12 m stage, in which the *Zauberflöte (Magic Flute)*, an opera in two acts with a libretto by the theatre director Emanuel Schikaneder, was performed for the first time on the 30th of September 1791. Mozart no longer lived to witness the triumphal procession of the masonic fairy tale opera which began soon after. In Vienna alone there were two hundred performances till 1798. There

VIENNA

were parallel productions in places like Prague, Frankfurt, Berlin, Hamburg, Dresden and Weimar. A post scriptum concerning the "Freihaus area": It was here that the so-called "Zauberflötenhäuschen" (the little Magic Flute house), a wooden shed, once stood, in which Mozart is supposed to have composed parts of his last opera. It has been in Salzburg since 1873 and can be found, since 1950, in the Bastionsgarden of the Museum (see: Salzburg, 15 Zauberflötenhäuschen).

43 St. Marxer Friedhof

(St. Marx Cemetery) (3., Leberstraße 6–8): This Gods acre is generally acknowledged as the world's last remaining Biedermeier cemetery with its many remarkable and interesting gravestones, and is as a whole under the protection of the Preservation Council. Even though, in the meantime, it is bypassed by the

Papageno – one of the classic figures of opera-literature.

Even though the St. Marx Cemetery, in Vienna's third district, is surrounded by motorways, it is, nevertheless, worth visiting because of its wonderful atmosphere.

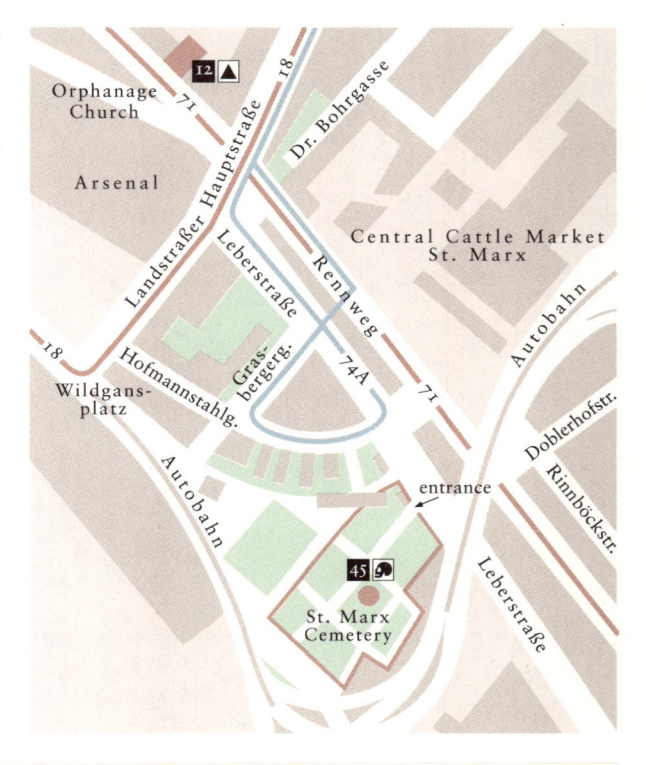

VIENNA

extremely busy south-east circular motorway, it has nevertheless kept its very special enchanting atmosphere. The "Mozart Grave" though, to be found a few paces left of the main path with the grave number 179, can correspond only roughly to the place where Mozart was really interred; following the hurried burial in a multiple grave, that was not only not marked in any way but was, furthermore, to be re-used after just a few years.

Apart from the fact that Mozart was nearly penniless at the time of his death, numerous legends

The site of the poetic memorial, in St. Marx Cemetery, corresponds only roughly with the location of the communal grave where Mozart's corpse was interred.

were beginning to form around this indignified funeral – his widow's miserliness, the disloyalty of his friends who neither accompanied him to his grave, nor found it neccessary to pay for a decent burial. In reality the way Mozart was buried on the evening of the 6th of December or the morning of the 7th – the exact time was not recorded – was completely according to the regulations of the Age of Enlightenment. Not only was the so-called third class funeral with a small cortège for 8 guilders and 56 farthings quite suitable for the majority of the Viennese public, it was also perfectly normal for someone with the social position of a musician – first and second class burials were considered a privilege reserved exclusively for the aristocracy and high-class citizens. The custom of using a multiple grave i.e. for a number of corpses, was not unusual either. And the fact that the funeral cortège – braving bad weather or not – not knowing the exact time of burial, did not go the whole way (a distance of 4 800 paces, that is 3,6 km) to the communal cemetery far beyond the city walls, but walked silently only to the city gate to bid farewell, was not unexpected and considered appropriate for those times, as was the absence of the widow. One definite exception to the rule was the funeral carriage that Constanze herself had ordered, following a suggestion that had been made by Gottfried van Swieten, for the transportation of her husband's body to the graveyard.

44 St. Michael

(1., Michaelerplatz): In the former court parish and Barnabite church of St. Michael, where the Cecilia Congregation of Court Musicians had its seat, "The Office for the dead was held for Wolfgang Amadeus Mozart, during which parts of his Requiem were heard for the first time" according to an inscription on the outer facade on December 10th 1791. The two theatre directors Emanuel Schikaneder and Joseph von Bauernfeld were to carry the costs. Just one year later the partly late-Romanesque, partly Gothic church received its Classical re-designed facade. There are two bronze plates in the right-hand doorway in remembrance of Mozart, which show a portrait and a skull.

Above the Papageno gate: Schikaneder in his favourite role with children.

The Papageno gate. Side entrance to the Theatre an der Wien.

45 THEATRE AN DER WIEN

with Papagenotor (6., Millöckergasse/Linke Wienzeile): Built in the years 1798-1801 for Emanuel Schikaneder, this was the biggest and most beautiful playhouse of its time. It was in his Freihaus-Theater, where Mozart and he had performed the *Magic Flute* together for the first time in 1791. The Theater an der Wien was to witness countless first performances: Beethoven's violin concerto resounded here for the first time, many works by the ingenious satirist Johann Nestroy, operettas by Johann Strauß (1874 the "Fledermaus"), Karl Millöcker, Karl Zeller and, after 1900, Franz Lehár, Emmerich Kálmán and Leo Fall; nowadays it has advanced to become a musical stage of European format. At the side entrance of the enchanting house, which was unfortunately partly demolished in 1902, one finds the famous "Papageno-Tor", showing the Principal together with children in his favourite role – as Papageno.

The illustration shows the theatre's former appearance, before the Vienna River was regulated.

VIENNA

46 LEHÁR-SCHIKANEDER-MANSION
(19., Hackhofergasse 18): Indirect homage is paid to Mozart here in this little palace in the noble villa district of Döbling. This house, today adapted as a museum, was not only the home of the creator of the "Merry Widow, "Land of Smiles" and other operetta evergreens (1932–44), but also – during the years 1802–12 – of the theatre director and *Magic Flute* libretto writer, Emanuel Schikaneder. Well worth seeing, apart from a few memorabilia, is the ceiling fresco by Vincenzio Sacchetti, brother of Lorenzo Sacchetti, the famous court theatre scene-painter. The fresco shows "the Queen of the night with the three ladies and Monostatos".

47 ZENTRALFRIEDHOF
(Central Cemetery) (11., Simmeringer Hauptstraße 234): "Dedicated by the City of Vienna 1859" – the inscription could hardly be any shorter. Does it reflect the bad conscience the public had towards the genius of geniuses? Even though it wasn't until the mid-fifties of the nineteenth-century, that the Vienna City Council was to make serious inquiries into

Vienna's Central Cemetery is the biggest Gods acre in the world. 24 sq. km. in surface area, roughly **300 000** graves and, till now, about **three million** burials.

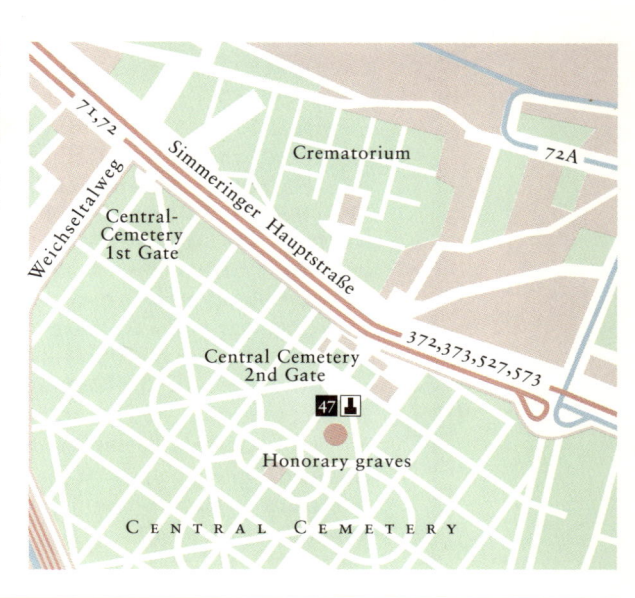

The honoury Mozart memorial, in the Central Cemetery, with the very short inscription: "Dedicated by the Vienna City Council 1859", further, No. 55/group 32A.

the whereabouts of Mozart's remains, and even then the results were not too accurate, at least the city's leaders saw occasion to erect the memorial that had been designed by Hans Gasser, on the site most likely to be the burial-place in St Marx, in the year 1859. In 1891, the year of the centenary of Mozart's death, the Muse leaning on a pile of books with her lyre and notes was moved to the honorary grave section of the Central Cemetery. And today, next to the honorary graves of Schubert, Beethoven, Brahms, Johann Strauß and many other composers, this is where it attracts thousands of Mozart-pilgrims every year as "Grave" number 55/group 32A.

48 Mozart Monument

(1., Burggarten): In 1898 a committee, established only with the one aim namely that of erecting a monument in honour of the great composer, commissioned the sculptor Viktor Tilgner with its design. The result that same year was a neo-Baroque statue with Mozart at the music- stand and at his feet laurel wreaths, musical instruments and putti; on the sides of the pedestal reliefs showing "Mozart as a child with his family" and "scenes from Don Giovanni". The original site was on the Albertinaplatz between the Opera and the Albrechtsrampe, but on the 12th of March 1945, during one of the last air-raids of World War II, it was badly damaged. After renovation it was to find a new home, in June 1953, in the Burggarten near the exit to the Babenbergerstraße.

Mozart's monument in the Burggarten. The work of Victor Tilgner, that stood on the Albertina Square till 1957.

The suburb of Wieden, today the 4th district of Vienna, used to be seperated from the city by the old walls.

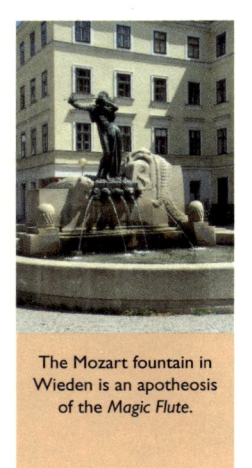

The Mozart fountain in Wieden is an apotheosis of the *Magic Flute*.

49 MOZART FOUNTAIN
(4., Mozartplatz): This fountain, which is often referred to as the Magic Flute fountain, was unveiled on October 8th 1905 on the quiet square between Favoriten- and Wiedner Hauptstraße. Designed entirely by O. Schöntal, but completed in bronze by the sculptor and medallion-maker Karl Wollek, it shows in abstract flowing forms the flute-playing Tamino and, leaning on him, Pamina, the daughter of the Queen of the Night.

50 STATE OPERA HOUSE
(1., Opernring 2): Here in the opera house built by August Siccardsburg und Eduard van der Nüll in Historicist style (1861–69) there are a number of rooms, where, during intermissions or

guided tours, the visitor may come across Mozart and his works: The artist Moritz von Schwind chose many motives from the *Magic Flute* for his fresco-cycle in the Loggia. In the Schwind Foyer there is a Mozart bust, above which the artist has painted a picture showing figures that appear in three of Mozart's operas *Le nozze di Figaro*, *Don Giovanni* and the *Magic Flute*. Last but not least upon entering the "Mahler-Saal" more figures from Mozart's final opera can be seen woven into the tapestries around the walls. The characters are: the Queen of the night, Papagena, Pamina, Papageno and Tamino.

51 GRIECHENBEISL
(1., Fleischmarkt 11): In what is presumably Vienna's oldest restaurant, dating back to 1490, and known until the end of the 18th century as "Zum roten Dachl", only later due to the many Greeks living in the vicinity given its present name, Mozart has left his very own hand-written signature. In the so-called Mark Twain- or Signature room, for centuries now, prominent guests from Mozart and Beethoven to Einstein and Gina Lollobrigida have taken the trouble to immortalize themselves by signing their names on the walls and ceiling.

Don Giovanni, the adulterer. Detail from a picture on the wall in the Schwind-Foyer, Vienna State Opera.

MOZART'S VIENNA – FACTS

Vienna city code: 0222 or 1
(International: +43-1-)

MUSEUMS, MEMORIALS AND GRAVE:

FIGARO HOUSE
(Mozart-Apartment): 1., Domgasse 5/
Schulerstraße 8 (Daily except Mon
9 a.m.–12:15 and 1–4:30 p.m.),
phone 513 62 94

STEFFL DEPARTMENT STORE
(Last Residence, Rauhensteingasse 8/
Kärntner Straße 19): Memorial in the
music department on the 5th floor
(Mon–Fri 9:30–7:30 p.m,
Sat 9–5:30 p.m.)

ST. STEPHAN'S CATHEDRAL
(Interior daily 6 a.m.–10 p.m.;
Guided tours Mon–Sat : 10:30 a.m.
and 3 p.m., Sun, public holidays
3 p.m., June to September also
Sat 7 p.m.,
phone 515 52-526

ST. MICHAEL'S CHURCH:
1., Michaelerplatz

AM HOF CHURCH
(former Church of the Jesuits):
1., Am Hof

ST. PETER'S CHURCH:
1., Petersplatz
(all: daily 7 a.m.–6 p.m.)

ST. MARX CEMETARY
(memorial grave) No. 179):
3., Leberstraße 6–8 (June–August
7 a.m.–7 p.m., May/September 7 a.m.–
6 p.m., October–April 7 a.m.–5 p.m.)

CENTRAL CEMETARY
(Grave No. 55, group 32 A):
11., Simmeringer Hauptstraße 234
(May–August 7 a.m.–7 p.m.,
March/April/Sept/October 7 a.m.–
6 p.m., November–February 8 a.m.–
5 p.m.) (both Tram 71 from Ring/
Schwarzenbergplatz; further
information: Council (MA 7),
phone 40000-84729 or MA 42,
phone 513 21 08

LÉHAR-SCHIKANEDER-MANSION:
19., Hackhofergasse 18 (by prior
arrangement only), phone 318 54 16

EVENTS (pre-booking):

STATE OPERA HOUSE:
1., Opernring 2, tickets at the
Federal theatre Box-office,
1., Hanuschgasse, courtyard (daily
8 a.m.–6 p.m.), phone 514 44-2955;
(Guided tours July/August daily
10, 11 a.m. 1, 2, 3 p.m.; and upon
request) phone 514 44-2613/2421

VOLKSOPER:
9., Währingerstraße 78, tickets – see
State Opera House

THEATRE AN DER WIEN
(Mozart Operas during the Vienna

Festival May/June): 6., Linke
Wienzeile 6, phone 588 30-588

Musik Verein:
1., Bösendorferstraße 12,
phone 505 81 90

Konzert House:
3., Lothringerstraße 20,
phone 712 46 86-0

Schönbrunn Palace – Puppet Theatre:
13., Schloß Schönbrunn, Hofrats wing, phone 817 32 47 (*Magic Flute* and other works)

Burg Chapel
(Mass with the Vienna Boys' Choir):
1., Hofburg, Schweizerhof (January–June and mid-September–December on Sundays and religious holidays 9:15 a.m.), phone 533 99 27; Postal bookings at least eight weeks prior apply: Hofmusikkapelle, Hofburg, A-1010 Vienna. Tickets, subject to availability, at the box office in the Chapel of the Imperial Palace each Friday between 4 and 6 p.m. for the following Sunday

House of the Teutonic Knights
(Vienna Concert Duo and Vienna Concert Quintet): 1., Singerstraße 7 (Duo: all year Mon–Fri and Sun 8 p.m., Sat 5 p.m. in the Sala terena; Quintet: Fri and Sun 6 p.m. inner court yard or concert hall),
phone 214 04 01, fax 216 71 42

Tickets for above mentioned events also available at ticket agencies.

ORIGINAL DOCUMENTS, NOTES, AUTOGRAPHS E.T.C.:

Historical Museum of the City of Vienna:
4., Karlsplatz (daily except Monday 9 a.m.-4:30 p.m.); phone 505 87 47

Museum of Fine Arts:
Collection of Ancient Musical
1., Neue Burg, Heldenplatz (daily except Tuesdays 10 a.m.–6 p.m.),
phone 525 24-0

Institute for Music University of Vienna:
1., Universitätsstraße 7,
phone 401 03-0

OTHERS:

Griechenbeisl
(original signature): 1., Fleischmarkt 11 (daily 11–1 a.m., dining till 11:30 p.m.), phone 533 19 41

AUSTRIA'S THEATRE MUSEUM:
1., Lobkowitzplatz 2 (daily except Monday 10 a.m.–5 p.m.; guided tours only upon request),
phone 512 88 00

NATIONAL LIBRARY
with Grand Hall: 1., Hofburg, entrance: Josephsplatz (end of May–end of October 10 a.m.–4 p.m., beginning of November–end of May 10 a.m.–12 noon; Attention: opening times do vary!)

SCHÖNBRUNN PALACE
(State apartments and Orangerie): 13., Schloß Schönbrunn (daily 8:30 a.m.–5 p.m.), phone 81113

MOZART COMMUNITY VIENNA:
2., Stuwerstraße 1–3,
phone 218 16 05 (728 16 05)

BOOK SHOPS WITH LITERATURE ON THE SUBJECT
(see also music stores)

AMADEUS:
6., Mariahilfers Straße 37–39,
phone 586 23 92-0

HARTLEBEN:
1., Walfischgasse 14,
phone 512 62 41

KUPPITSCH:
1., Schottengasse 4 and Herrengasse 14,
phone 533 32 68 and 533 32 68-20

MUSIK MÜLLER:
1., Krugerstraße 4, phone 512 28 75

ÖSTERREICHISCHER BUNDESVERLAG:
1., Schwarzenbergstraße 5,
phone 512 29 63

ZENTRALBUCHHANDLUNG:
1., Schulerstraße 1–3,
phone 512 69 05

MUSIC STORES:

ARCADIA
(Opera shop in the State Opera): 1., Staatsoper/Kärntner Straße,
phone 513 95 68

MUSIKHAUS DOBLINGER
(also CDs and both new and second-hand notes): 1., Dorotheergasse 10,
phone 515 03-0

CLASSIC-CDS
(see also Music stores):

EMI AUSTRIA:
1., Kärntner Straße 30,
phone 512 36 75-77

GRAMOLA:
1., Kohlmarkt 5 and Graben 16,
phone 533 50 47 and 533 50 34

HAVLICEK:
1., Herrengasse 5, phone 533 19 64

SCHALLPLATTEN-WIEGE:
1., Graben 29a, phone 533 20 32

TEUCHTLER (ANTIQUARIAN):
6., Windmühlgasse 10
(Mon–Fri 1 p.m.–6 p.m., Sat 10 a.m.–12 noon),
phone 586 21 33

VIRGIN:
6., Mariahilfer Straße 37–39, phone 588 37-0

COFFEE HOUSES:

BRÄUNERHOF:
1., Stallburggasse 2 (Mon–Fri 7:30 a.m.–7:30 p.m., Sat 7:30 a.m.–6 p.m., Sun 10 a.m.–6 p.m.), phone 512 38 93

CENTRAL:
1., Herrengasse/Strauchgasse (Mon–Sat 9 a.m.–8 p.m.), phone 533 37 63-26

DEMEL:
1., Kohlmarkt 14 (daily 10 a.m.–6 p.m.), phone 533 55 16-0

DIGLAS:
1., Wollzeile 10 (Mon–Sat 7 a.m.–12 midnight; Sun, public holidays 10 a.m.–12 midnight), phone 512 84 01

DOM-CAFÉ:
1., Stephansplatz 9 (daily 10:30 a.m.–10 p.m.), phone 534 05-0

DOMMAYER:
13., Auhofstraße 2/Dommayergasse (daily 7 a.m.–12 midnight), phone 877 54 65

FRAUENHUBER:
1., Himmelpfortgasse 6 (Mon–Fri 8 a.m.-11 p.m., Sat 8 a.m.-4 p.m.), phone 512 43 65

HAWELKA:
1., Dorotheergasse 6 (Wed–Mon 8 a.m.–2 a.m., Sun and public holidays 4 p.m.–2 a.m.), phone 512 82 30

LANDTMANN:
1., Dr. Karl-Lueger-Ring 4 (daily 8 a.m.–12 midnight), phone 532 06 21

SACHER:
1., Philharmonikerstraße 4 (daily 6:30 a.m.–11:30 p.m.), phone 514 56

SPERL:
6., Gumpendorfer Straße 11 (Mon–Sat 7 a.m.–11 p.m., Sun except July/August 3–11 p.m.), phone 586 41 58

GENERAL INFORMATION FOR TOURISTS:

TOURIST-INFORMATION:
Information-City – 1., Kärntner Straße 38 (daily 9 a.m.–7 p.m.), phone 513 88 92; Information-Süd: 10., Triester Straße 149 (April/May/October daily 9 a.m.–7 p.m., July-September daily 8 a.m.–10 p.m.), phone 616 00 70; Information-West: 14., Auhof (April-October daily 8 a.m.–10 p.m., November daily 9 a.m.–7 p.m., Dec.–March daily 10 a.m.–6 p.m.),

phone 979 12 71; also at the Airport, Vienna-Schwechat, and West and South train stations

FURTHER INFO.:
Rathaus-/City-Info.: 1., Rathaus, Friedrich-Schmidt-Platz
(Mon–Fri 8 a.m.–6 p.m.),
phone 403 89 89.
Vienna Tourist Board – 2., Obere Augartenstr. 40
(Mon–Fri 8 a.m.–5 p.m.),
phone 21114-0.
Austria Info.: 4., Margaretenstr. 1/ corner Wiedner Hauptstr.
(Mon–Wed and Fri 9 a.m.–5:30 p.m., Thu 9 a.m.–6 p.m.),
phone 587 20 00

GUIDED WALKING TOURS:
On a wide variety of themes, including musical, duration about 1 1/2 hours, minimum 3 people. No prior reservations required.
For information:
phone 514 50-243 or 894 53 63

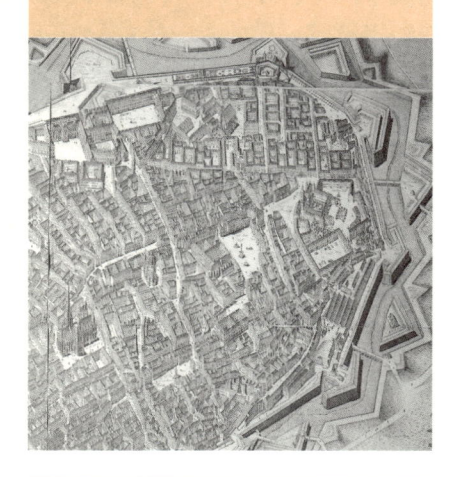

MORE
MOZART MEMORIALS

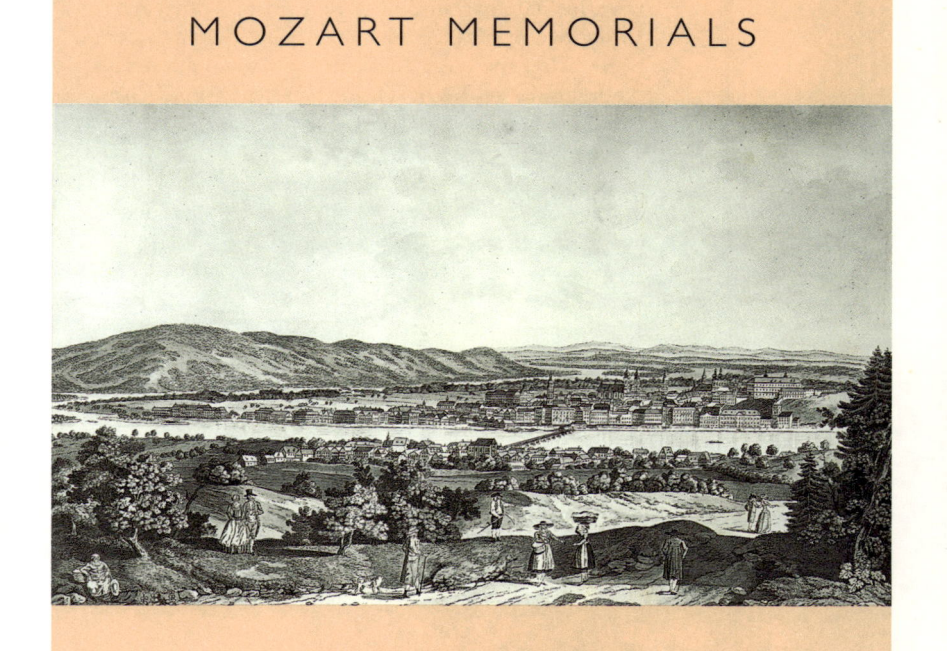

Melk Abbey

On their autumn journey from Salzburg to Vienna the Mozarts stopped, in the year 1767, on the 14th September, at the famous Benedictine Abbey. After the midday meal in town they went "up to the abbey", as Leopold father relates, where they "looked at the rooms" and "didn't identify ourselves until, in the church, Wolfgang played the organ and the organist had the chance to recognize or guess who he was ... We were off in the coach straight after on our way to St. Pölten".

In 1768 a second stay was made at the Abbey and on the 28th December the prior was to make a note in his diary: "At 6 'o' clock Mr Mozart arrived with his wife, his daughter and his famous son, who at the tender age of only 12, has already excelled as a composer. After the boy had played the organ admirably, the honourable Regens chori suggested a luncheon should be prepared outside. The honourable Abbot was present at the meal." And the diary entry made the next day: "Mr. Mozart ('Kapellmeister' from Salzburg) and his family left at 7:15 a.m. He travels to Linz in a coach and four."

Facsimiles of these diary notes are exhibited in the rooms open to the public.

The Abbey of Melk: built by Jakob Prandtauer, reigning supreme above the Danube. This centre of religious worship guards the entrance to the Wachau.

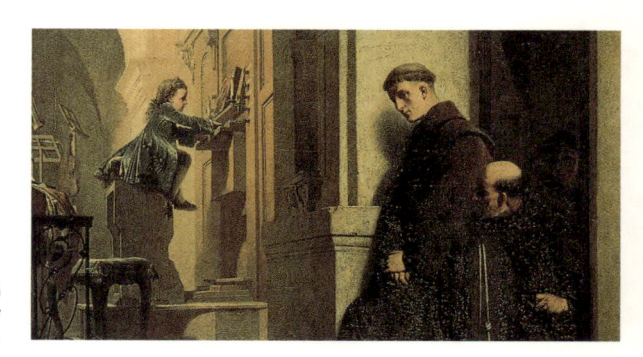

"Mozart at the organ in Ybbs", painted by Heinrich Lossow, 1864.

Ybbs

At midday on October 5th 1762 Leopold, Nannerl and Wolfgang made a stop at Ybbs on their boat trip from Linz to Vienna. Whilst travelling companions from the clergy celebrated Mass, Wolfgang, his father wrote in a letter, "romped about and played the organ in the Fransiscan Church so well, that when the Franciscan friars, who were sat eating their midday meal with guests, heard him, they jumped up from their seats, left their food and, together with their guests, ran into the choir and were so astonished they nearly died". The former monastery has served the City of Vienna for decades now as a centre for therapy and nursing, however the above mentioned church still remains open to the institution's inmates and any other member of the public during Sunday morning Mass. The organ that the six-year-old played so enthusiastically, is found today in the church of the Carthusian monastery at Gaming. Anyone strolling along the so-called promenade can find a plaque, on the outside wall of the establishment, recording the sensational short-performance that Mozart gave here. In the former city museum in the Herrengasse there is a furnished "Mozart-room" with a number of facsimiles documenting the different aspects of Mozart's life. Also on show is a copy of the picture by Heinrich Lossow – the 1864 original is in the depot of Upper Austria's provincial museum in Linz – which captures the moment, in the manner of the 19th century, when the monks listen in awe to the little key-board magician.

The city of Ybbs is an obligatory stop on a Danube trip.

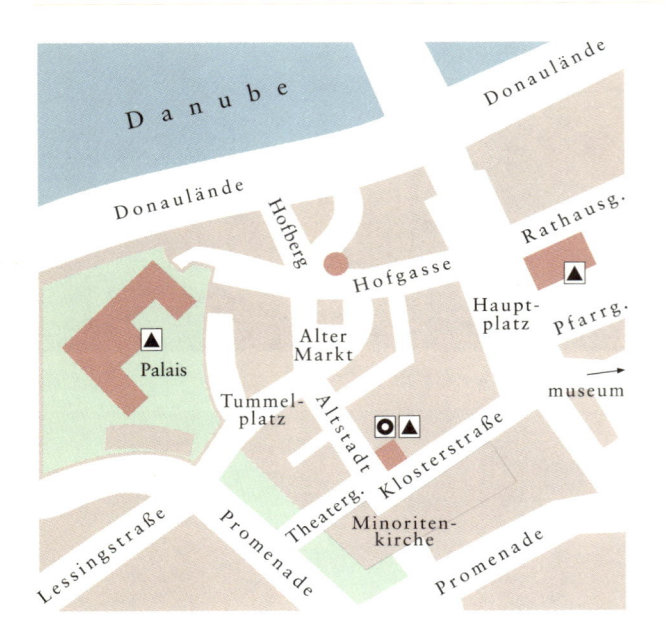

The Linz Cathedral. Mozart probably stayed with the chorister for ten days in 1790.

LINZ

The Mozarts always made a stop in the capital of Upper Austria on their numerous journeys between Salzburg and Vienna. In November 1783 they were the guests of Johann Joseph Anton Count Thun, in whose house they were "treated with so much courtesy" for three weeks in all. On this occasion Wolfgang composed, "head over heels" because he didn't have a finished one ready, a new symphony, the so-called *Linzer in C major (K 425)* (for a concert he gave on the 4th November in the local "Wassertheater"). The *piano sonata in B major (K 333)*, named *the Linzer sonata* was most probably also composed at this time aswell.

The Starhemberg house of Count Thun (former Altstadt No. 17, today: Klosterstraße 20) has a niche in the entrance where, since 1983, there has been a bronze bust of Mozart by the local sculptor Walter Ritter.

And opposite, in the entrance hall, there is a marble plaque as a reminder of the composer's stay. The

MORE MOZART MEMORIALS 162

memorial room that was once open to visitors is now, unfortunately, closed.

Another memorial site with a commemorative plaque is the former tavern that belonged to the Kiener Family "Zur Dreifaltigkeit" (The Holy Trinity) (Hofgasse 14/Hofberg 11), where the Mozarts stayed in October 1762. Still in existence is the festival hall in today's Rathaus, where Wolfgang – in all probability – gave a concert on October 1st 1762 under the patronage of the provincial commissioner Count Leopold Schlick.

Among the collection of manuscripts, which is only shown on special request, in the posession of the provincial museum, there is the funny poem titled "Glückwunsch beim Punsch" (congratulations over a glass of punch), that Wolfgang sent to Nannerl on the 31st July, 1783 and Constanze gave to the Linz museum society as a present.

Lambach Abbey

On their trips to and from Vienna the Mozart family, documented by the various letters, were in Lambach at least four times: September 12th 1767, early January 1769, late September 1773 and late October 1783. The reason: Leopold Mozart had in younger years, whilst at Salzburg university, made friends with Amandus Schickmayr, a man of about his

The Abbey Theatre in Lambach – the only one still in existance in the whole of Austria.

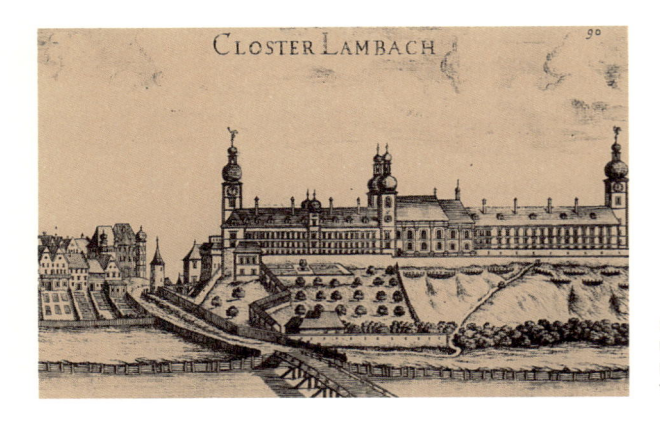

Lambach Abbey in Upper Austria, as seen by Georg Matthäus Vischer in 1674.

age. This gentleman was in office as Abbot of the venerable Lambach Abbey from 1746 till 1794 and was, as such, a great lover of music. In Lambach emphasis had always been on the care of musical tradition: not only did the Abbey have a small orchestra but it also had its own theatre, which, by the way, is the only, still existing, Baroque abbey-theatre in all Austria.

Leopold Mozart presented Abbot Amandus with a gift of the manuscripts of fifteen of his symphonies. And Wolfgang Amadeus even dedicated a piece to the abbey, the *"Jugendsymphonie" in G major (K 45a)*, also known as the *Old Lambacher symphony*. There will be a permanent exhibition installed in the foyer of the theatre during this coming year, next to the guest wing where the Mozarts used to stay, with reproductions of pictures and a facsimile of the score of the *symphony in G major*, the original of which has, unfortunately, disappeared.

St. Gilgen

In today's county court (Ischlerstraße 15) in the holiday resort on the west shore of the Wolfgangsee, on the 25th December, 1720 Mozart's mother, Anna Maria Walburga Pertl, was born. Her father, Wolfgang Nikolaus Pertl, had studied at St. Peter's college in Salzburg and had appeared as a singer. He became a lawyer, and in 1716 was appointed curator of St. Gilgen. About 1720 he had the derelict public assistance house, today's regional court house, rebuilt.

Mozart's mother was baptised in the local parish church of St. Aegidius. She lived in her home town till her father died in 1724, then moved with her mother and her sister to Salzburg, where she married the violinist Leopold Mozart from Augsburg. Of the seven children they had, only two, Maria Anna Walburga Ignatia, called "Nannerl", and Wolfgang Amadeus, survived.

On the 23rd of August 1784 Mozart's sister married Prince Johann Baptist Berchtold zu Sonnenburg. This gentleman, who was fifteen years older than her, succeeded her grandfather in office. Together with him and his five children she moved back to St. Gilgen – to the house of her mother. When she, in the meantime a mother of three herself, became a widow in 1801, she moved back to Salzburg.

In 1983 the Mozarteum Foundation opened a small memorial site in the historical building, which besides its authenticity, a few facsimiles and copies of pictures concerning the history of the family and the house in a 3 × 4 m sized room, offers little to the visitor. The neighbouring local museum on the Wetzl-Einsiedlerhaus (Pichlerplatz 6), houses – for the time being – a worthwhile light and sound show about "Mozart's journeys". And in the parish church, in front of the stairs to the choir, there is a plaque commemorating the "wedding of W. A. Mozart's grandparents on 22. 11. 1712, the christening of his mother on 25. 12. 1720, the burial of his grandfather on 9. 3. 1724, the wedding of his sister on 23. 8. 1784 and the burial of his brother-in-law on the 2. 3. 1801".

The Mozart fountain in St. Gilgen, on Lake Wolfgang. Erected in memory of Mozart's relatives.

Maria Plain

To the north of Salzburg, on a high vantage point, reigns a pilgrimage church where the Mozarts often had masses celebrated. Wolfgang loved to go up to the picturesque twin-steepled building to improvise on the organ. The story that he composed the *Coronation Mass in C major (K 317)*, in 1779 for the church's jubilee celebration of the crowning of the

A contemporary engraving of Maria Plain. The pilgrimage church towers over the city on the Salzach. Engraving by Philipp Kilian, late 17th century.

miraculous image, even though it may meet the romantic desire of history, is most probably only a myth. Nevertheless the magnificent piece is played up here every year on the 15th August: the first time it was ever heard was on Easter Sunday 1779 down in the valley, in Salzburg Cathedral. What was quite certainly composed for Maria Plain, however, was in fact the *Missa brevis in D major (K 194)* for the centennial celebration of the consecration of the church. This piece was performed for the first time in August of 1774.

BADEN

Throughout the years 1773, 1784, 1789, 1790 and 1791 Mozart had repeatedly made trips to the idyllic town on the edge of the Vienna Woods – mostly to visit friends and in the last two years, to see Constanze, who was here hoping to relieve her foot ailment by bathing at the spa. After his first visit in 1783, Leopold, Mozart's father, noted pleasantly surprised: "Baden is a little town. There are many baths; everything is much as it is in Gastein, only quite a lot more comfortable."

One Mozart-room, used during the summer of his last year, remains identifiable: Constanze was staying at the house "Zum Blumenstock" (to the Flower Plant) (Renngasse No. 29, today: No. 4) and her husband was to rent a small attic room in the extension built onto the court. This was where he wrote the piece which is no doubt his most famous sacred work: the motet *Ave Verum (K 618)*, most likely for the local teacher and regens chori Anton Stoll, on the eve of the 18th June 1791. Where the original house once stood is today's "Mozart-Hof", built in 1885/86, and since 1977 home to a special hospital for rheumatism-suffering agrarians. A memorial plaque adorns the facade of the building. Since 1911 there is a second inscription to be found at the entrance to the stairs leading to the choir of the Baden parish church of St. Stephan's. It is a dedication from the local society for church-music in remembrance of the creation of the *Ave Verum*. In a three-dimensional fashion one encounters the prominent short-stay visitor in the Spa park, to be exact: in the middle of the so-called Mozart temple, where a bust of the Maestro stands on a pedestal. There is another bust one can see in the city's Rollett museum standing next to a coloured lithography (copied from a photograph) of Mozart's old quarters in the Renngasse.

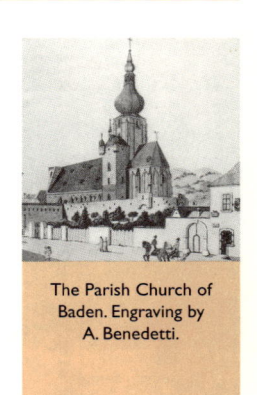

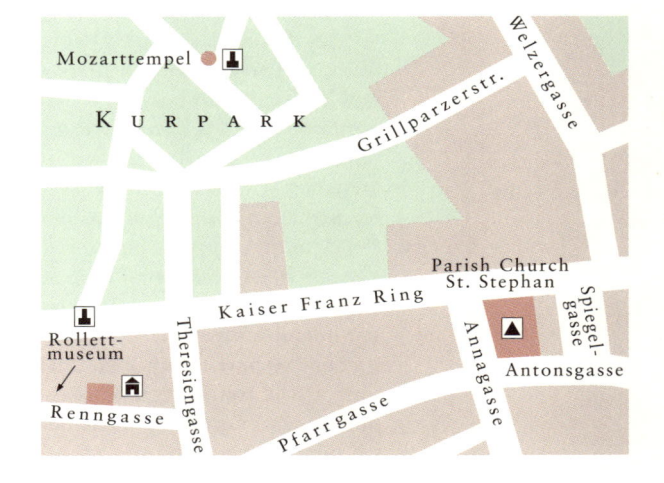

The Parish Church of Baden. Engraving by A. Benedetti.

MORE MOZART MEMORIALS

The only Freemason museum in the whole of Austria can be found in the Baroque Castle of Rosenau in the Waldviertel.

SCHLOSS ROSENAU

In the Baroque palace, about 10 km west of Zwettl, which was rebuilt betwen 1730–40 by Leopold Christoph Count Schallenberg, the only Freemason museum in Austria can be found. Among the numerous exhibits in the permanent collection there are several relating to Mozart who, as the most famous Brother in the history of this humanitarian society, not only composed many "masonic" works, but also, supported by Joseph II, played an important leading role in the social fight for equality for freelance artists. On show is, amongst other items, the printed copy of the circular sent by the Lodge "Zur Wohltätigkeit" in December 1784, where "Kapellmeister" Mozart's forthcoming membership is announced to the Sister Lodges; further, the membership list of the Lodge "Zur neugekrönten Hoffnung", in which Mozart's name appears; the theatre page of the first performance of the masonic opera *The Magic Flute;* a copper frontispiece of the cantata *Masonic Joy (K 471)* and an oil painting showing the "interior of a Viennese Lodge", with most probably Mozart and Schikaneder at the front.

ET CETERA

Indefatigable detectives can moreover find more at Stuppach Castle, roughly 100 km south of Vienna. On the north-eastern edge of the city of Gloggnitz, stands, freshly renovated, the Castle of Stuppach, once the manorial domain of Count Franz von Walsegg-Stuppach, the man who, in a pretty ominous manner, commissioned Mozart to compose the *Requiem* in July of 1791. In nearby Wiener Neustadt a visit should be paid to the church of the former Dominican Neukloster. Because it was here that Count Stuppach had the *Requiem* – after it had already been performed under Mozart's name in Vienna – played for the first time as his own composition and under his own direction on February 14th 1794. The performance was repeated two months later at the foot of the Semmering mountain, in the pilgrimage church of Maria Schutz, which was under Count Stuppach's patronage. And finally, 400 km away in Innsbruck, a memorial worthy of mention – on the facade of the former tavern "Zum weißen Kreuz" (the white cross) (Herzog-Friedrich-Straße 31), there is a plaque commemorating the overnight stay Mozart made here, on his way to Italy, on December the 15th 1769.

This was the secret messenger (who inspired biographers and illustrators to make fanciful interpretations) who brought Mozart the commission, for the *Requiem*, that had come from Count Franz von Stuppach.

MINOR MEMORIALS – FACTS

MELK

BENEDICTINE ABBEY OF MELK: A-3390 Melk, Abt-Berthold-Dietmayr-Straße 1. Open for tours from Palm Sunday till 1st November with or without a guide (April and October 9 a.m.–5 p.m., May till September 9 a.m.–6 p.m.; entrance until one hour before closing; guided tours on the hour). From the 1st November till Palm Sunday only at 11 a.m. and 2 p.m. for guided tours (advance bookings for groups 9 a.m. –4 p.m.). Besides the "Baroque Days" at Whitsuntide (Sat–Mon) organ recitals are held in the Abbey Church on Ascension Day and Corpus Christi as well as late evening on the 15th August. Organ concerts: phone 02752/ 2312.

YBBS

Mozart Hall in the former city museum (Herrengasse 23). Open to the public from Easter till the 1st of November, on Wednesdays from 3–5 p.m. Or by prior arrangement, phone 07412/526/120.

LAMBACH

Benedictine Abbey Lambach: A-4650 Lambach, Klosterplatz 1 Open daily from Easter Monday till the 1st of November, guided tours at 2 p.m. through the abbey (duration c. 1 1/2 hrs. includes the church, Romanesque fresco paintings in the west choir, ambulatory, summer refectory, library and theatre). Guided tours, for groups of 15 or more, all year round at 9:00, 9:30, 10 a.m., 2:00 or 3:30 p.m. can be booked by prior arrangement, phone: 07245/217 10-0.

LINZ

Castle museum (permanent exhibition): 4010 Linz, Tummelplatz 10 (Tue–Fri 9 a.m.–5p.m., Sat, Sun10 a.m.–4 p.m.), phone: 0732/77 44 19. Museum of the Province of Upper Austria (temporary exhibition): 4010 Linz, Museumstraße 14 (Tue–Fri 9 a.m.–6 p.m. Sat, Sun 10 a.m.–5 p.m.), phone: 0732/77 44 82-0.

ST. GILGEN

Mozart memorial in the district law-court house: A-5340 St. Gilgen, Ischlerstraße 15 (daily, except Mondays, from the 1st of June till the 30th of September between 10 a.m. –12 noon and 2–6 p.m.). Local history museum: im Wetzl-Einsiedlerhaus, Pichlerplatz 6 (same opening times as the memorial); for further information phone: 06227/348.

MARIA PLAIN

Pilgrims Church (3 km north east of Salzburg's city limits): open daily in summer from 8 a.m. to about 8 p.m., in winter till about 5 p.m.; adjoining abbey: phone: 0662/450 194.

Mozart went to Baden quite often. He went to see friends there, or to visit his wife who was frequently at the Spa for health reasons. The picture shows the main square with the Trinity Column in the middle. Painting by E. Gurk

BADEN

Rollett Museum und City Archive: A-2500 Baden, Weikersdorferplatz 1 (open daily except Tue 3–6 p.m.), phone: 02252/48 255.

ROSENAU

Freemason Museum in Rosenau Castle: A-3924 Rosenau. Open daily from Easter till the 1st of November, 9 a.m.–5 p.m., phone: 02822/8221.

SELECT BIBLIOGRAPHY

BECKER, MAX (Hg.): *Mozart. Sein Leben und seine Zeit in Texten und Bildern.* Insel, Frankfurt – Leipzig 1991

BRAUNBEHRENS, VOLKMAR: *Mozart in Wien.* Piper, München 1986

BUNDESPRESSEDIENST ÖSTERREICHS (Hg.): *Wolfgang Amadeus Mozart – 5. Dezember 1991: 200. Todestag.* Wien 1990

DUDÁK, VLADISLAV: *Der Wanderer durch Prag oder: Prag von allen Seiten.* Baset, Prag 1995

GOES, ALBRECHT (Hg.): *Mozart Briefe.* Fischer, Frankfurt a. M. 1979

GREITHER, ALOYS: *Mozart.* Rowohlt, Hamburg 1962

HILDESHEIMER, WOLFGANG: *Mozart.* Suhrkamp, Frankfurt a. M. 1977

HISTORISCHES MUSEUM DER STADT WIEN (Hg.): *Wolfgang Amadeus Mozart.* Wien o. J.

HISTORISCHES MUSEUM DER STADT WIEN (Hg.): *Zaubertöne. Mozart in Wien 1781–1791.* Katalog zur Ausstellung im Künstlerhaus 1990/91. Wien 1990

INTERNATIONALE STIFTUNG MOZARTEUM (Hg.): *W. A. Mozart – Neue Ausgabe sämtlicher Werke.* Salzburg o. J.

INTERNATIONALE STIFTUNG MOZARTEUM u. LAND SALZBURG (Hg.): *Mozart – Bilder und Klänge.* Katalog zur Landesausstellung 1991. Salzburg 1991

KADEŘÁBEK, RUDOLF: *In Prag war er glücklich.* Dialog, A. G., Prag 1991

KNEPLER, GEORG: *Wolfgang Amadé Mozart – Annäherungen.* Henschel, Berlin 1991

KÖCHEL, LUDWIG RITTER VON: *Chronologisch-thematisches Verzeichnis sämtlicher Tonwerke Wolfgang Amadé Mozarts.* 8. unveränderte Auflage. Wiesbaden 1983

KRETSCHMER, HELMUT: *Mozarts Spuren in Wien.* J & V, Wien 1990

LANDON, HOWARD C. ROBBINS (Hg.): *Das Mozart Kompendium. Sein Leben – seine Musik.* Droemer Knaur, München 1991

MÜLLER VON ASOW, E. H. (Hg.): *Wolfgang Amadeus Mozart – Verzeichnis aller meiner Werke u. Leopold Mozart – Verzeichnis der Jugendwerke W. A. Mozarts.* Doblinger, Wien – München 1956

NATIONALTHEATER IN PRAG (Hg.): *Das Ständetheater – Ein Führer durch das Gebäude.* Prag 1994

NEBEHAY, CHRISTIAN M.: *Wien Speziell – Musik der Klassik.* Brandstätter, Wien 1985

NEUE BADENER BLÄTTER: *Wolfgang Amadeus Mozart und Baden.* Gesellschaft der Freunde Badens und Städt. Sammlungen, Baden 1991

NOVELLO, MARY UND VINCENT: *Eine Wallfahrt zu Mozart – Die Reisetagebücher von V. und M. Novello aus dem Jahr 1829.* Darmstadt 1959

PARNASS, DIE ÖSTERR. KUNST- UND KULTURZEITSCHRIFT (Sonderheft): *Mozart.* Linz 1991

REMUS, MATTHIAS: *Mozart. Parkland,* Stuttgart 1991

SCHENK, ERICH: *Mozart – Eine Biographie.* Schott/Piper, Mainz 1989

VOLEK, TOMISLAV ET AL.: *Mozarts Opern für Prag.* Theaterinstitut (Hg.), Prag 1991

WEIKERT, ALFRED: *Musik-Spaziergang in Wien.* Berger, Horn/Wien o. J.

WITESCHNIK, ALEXANDER: *„Ihr Edler von Sauschwanz" oder: Mozart in Geschichten und Anekdoten.* Neff, Wien 1987

LIST OF ILLUSTRATIONS:

Austrian Archives, Vienna: Page 8 above and centre, 9 above, 10, 11 above, 15, 18 below, 12, 14 below, 21, 22, 24, 25 above, 26, 29 below, 31, 33, 37 above, 38 above, 39 below, 40 above and centre, 42 below, 44 above, 45 above, 46 above, 47 below, 48 below, 55, 57 centre, 62 above, 63, 64, 89, 90, 92, 93, 97, 99 below, 101 above, 102, 115, 125, 130, 136, 137, 139, 140, 144 centre, 169.

Picture Archives of the Austrian National Library, Vienna: Page 11 below, 18 below, 35 above, 44 below, 45 below.

City of Vienna Museum of History: Page 148 below.

International Foundation Mozarteum Salzburg: Page 8 above, 9 centre, 16, 20, 23 above and centre, 25 centre, 30 below, 38 below, 39 above, 49 centre, 57 below, 58 above, 73, 79, 118, 155.

Manfred Horvath, Vienna: Page 49 above, 56 above, 57 above, 58 below, 61 below, 66, 69, 70, 72, 74, 75, 76, 82, 116, 123 below, 160, 161, 168.

Janos Kalmar, Vienna: Page 88, 103 below, 105.

Museum of Fine Art, Vienna: Page 13.

Dagmar Landova, Vienna: Page 19, 124, 134 above, 146, 148 above and centre, 151, 151, 152.

Austrian National Tourism Board: Page 36, 59 above, 60, 61, 62 below, 65, 71, 117 below, 134 below, 157.

Christian Brandstätter Publishers, Vienna: Page 28 above, 37 centre and below, 40 below, 41, 49 below, 77, 91, 108, 113, 114, 119, 121, 122, 123 above, 127, 128, 131, 132, 141, 143, 144 above and below, 145 above, 153, 158, 159, 162, 163, 164, 166, 171.

Kurt-Michael Westermann, Vienna and Hamburg: Page 98, 101 centre and below, 103 above, 106, 107, 165.

Hans Wiesenhofer, Vienna: 135 below, 138 below.

Page 7: "The socalled Lime-Tree Avenue in the Augarten in Vienna". A coloured etching by Johann Ziegler, 1783.

Page 55: A model of Salzburg by Johann Rupert Fontaine, about 1790.

Page 85: Prague around 1800. An anonymous etching.

Page 113: Vienna, a view from the Belvedere. Painting by Bernado Bellotto (Canaletto) about 1760.

Page 159: A view of the city of Linz.

175

1st Edition

Layout and jacket design by fuhrer
Printed by Druckhaus Grasl, Bad Vöslau, Austria
Editor of the German version: Barbara Sternthal

Copyright © 1997 by Christian Brandstätter Verlagsgesellschaft m. b. H.
All rights reserved. This book may not be reproduced or transmitted, in whole or in part, in any form or by any means, electronic or mechanical, including photocopy, translations, recording, microfilm or any other information storage and retrieval system, without prior written permission from the Christian Brandstätter Verlagsgesellschaft m.b.H.
ISBN 3-85447-729-5
Christian Brandstätter Verlagsgesellschaft m.b.H.
A-1080 Wien, Wickenburggasse 26
Telephon (+43-1) 408 38 14